Stephan Schiffman's

101

SUCCESSFUL SALES STRATEGIES

Top Techniques to Boost Sales Today

ADAMS MEDIA

AVON, MASSACHUSETTS

Published by
Adams Media,
an F+W Publications Company
57 Littlefield Street, Avon, MA 02322. U.S.A.
www.adamsmedia.com

ISBN: 1-59337-376-7

Printed in the United States of America.

J I H G F E D C B A

Library of Congress Cataloging-in-Publication Data

Schiffman, Stephan.
Stephan Schiffman's 101 successful sales strategies : top techniques to boost sales
today /
by Stephan Schiffman.
p. cm.
Includes bibliographical references.
ISBN 1-59337-376-7
1. Selling. I. Title: Stephan Schiffman's one hundred one successful sales strategies.
II. Title.

HF5438.25.B33388 2005
658.8'2–dc22
2005017375

This publication is designed to provide accurate and authoritative information with
regard to the subject matter covered. It is sold with the understanding that the pub-
lisher is not engaged in rendering legal, accounting, or other professional advice. If
legal advice or other expert assistance is required, the services of a competent professional person should be sought.

—From a *Declaration of Principles* jointly adopted by a
Committee of the American Bar Association and a
Committee of Publishers and Associations

Many of the designations used by manufacturers and sellers to distinguish their product
are claimed as trademarks. Where those designations appear in this book and Adams
Media was aware of a trademark claim, the designations have been printed with initial
capital letters.

Contents

Introduction

This book is the result of more than a quarter of a century of front-line selling experience. I think you will find that it is a good deal more comprehensive than other books on selling.

The volume you are holding in your hands is not a cure-all; it doesn't promise an instant turnaround to your sales career the moment you start turning its pages. With out your efforts and your commitment to your own results, no book can realistically make that promise to you. Like any other blueprint for success, this one requires action on your part to put its ideas into practice.

I do, however, want to share my strong belief with you that if you make a concerted effort to follow the 101 "commandments" laid out here, and use the book as a kind of checklist as you move forward, you will be measurably more successful a year from now than you are today.

The Winning Edge

If you've ever watched the Olympic swimming, running, or bobsled competitions, you've no doubt noticed that the winners of these races tend to win by very slim margins—tenths or hundredths of a second. That's remarkable, isn't it? When the top athletes in the field come together, the amount of time that determines the gold medal is often about as much time as it takes to snap your fingers.

I think sales is sometimes very similar. The competition out there can be brutal. Victories are often decided by hairsbreadth margins. Lose three or four important races in a row by the tiniest of margins, and you're out of business; win three or four, and you're tops in your field.

The advice that follows is designed to help you add to your personal sales efficiency—a little bit here, a little bit there. I'm not out to reinvent the wheel with this book, but rather to give you enough of an edge in enough common problem areas to make victory more likely for you in a tough race.

Sometimes, when people first encounter some of the ideas you're about to see, they discount them immediately by saying something like this: "But that's so simple, so obvious!" When I hear that, I ask two questions:

1. Was it "obvious" before you read what you read?
2. Is it "simple" enough for you to implement on a daily or weekly basis after reading what you read?

You won't find long discourses on psychology or personal interaction here, but rather tangible, pragmatic ideas you can put into practice without a lot of research or second-guessing. If that's the kind of advice you're eager to get—reliable, easy-to-implement insider advice culled from a lifetime of face-to-face selling—read on.

Stephan Schiffman
New York, NY

Acknowledgments

I would like to thank the following people for their help with this book: Brandon Toropov, Michele Reisner, Gary Krebs, Danielle Chiotti, and, of course, Anne, Daniele, and Jennifer for their unceasing support.

Strategy #1

Be Obsessed

You must like what you are doing for a living—selling—enough to become obsessed with it. Not fifteen-hours-a-day obsessed; rather, I-have-absolutely-got-to-do-this-right-day-in-and-day-out obsessed.

For my money, the most crucial word in sales today is *obsession*. Close behind it are two supporting ideas, *utilization* and *implementation*. Let's talk a little bit about what these three words really mean for you.

Obsession

Every day I'm not training, I make fifteen dials. And by making fifteen dials, I can get through to maybe seven people. Once I get through to seven people, I'll usually set up one appointment. I do that five days a week, which, by extension, means that every week I have, on average, five new sales appointments. I close one out of five, so at the end of the year, I should have fifty new customers.

I mention my daily routine—my obsession, if you will, my repetitive, second nature approach to sales—so that you'll know I'm not just talking theory here. Many sales books are written by people who have retired or gotten out of business. I have not retired. I'm too young to retire, and I'm having too much fun to get out of business. I am an active, professional salesperson. I also happen to be president of one of the country's top sales training firms. Part of the reason for our success is that the people we work with know that we practice exactly what we preach, day in and day out.

In order for you to be successful in sales, you must be absolutely, positively obsessed with your work while you're doing it. You have to be so dedicated to the idea that you can satisfy a customer with your product or service that you move into a whole new work realm: A realm where there is simply no place for watching the clock, wishing it were time for a coffee break, or wondering how the Jets are going to do against the Patriots this Sunday. That's not to say there's no place for any of these things in your life—just that there's no place for any of these things while you're working. Now, this doesn't mean you must take yourself so seriously that you become a workaholic and have a heart attack at thirty-eight. It means you must make a commitment to yourself, and build up a routine that is success-oriented.

Of course, we should note here that obsession without discipline often results in chaos. As obsessive as you want to get about being successful, all that energy must be coupled with discipline or you're not going to get anywhere.

Utilization

This means utilizing everything at your disposal to increase your success. In a way, it's being obsessive about getting the most from your environment.

Burrow through company brochures and catalogs to learn everything you can about your product. Have regular meetings with your sales manager to discuss your performance and get new ideas. Use books like this one, or motivational tapes, to put you on the right track. In short, utilize your tools!

Such tools needn't be limited to things you can hold in your hand. Have you shown customers your office or plant? Have you reviewed past company successes with your prospect? Have you invited current and potential clients to company social outings? Be creative. Once you stop to think about it, you'll be amazed at how many excellent tools go completely ignored by salespeople.

Implementation

Or, if you prefer, just do it; make the effort in the first place. All the sales books in the world will not help you if you don't try.

Don't fall prey to the "paralysis of analysis." One of the beautiful things about sales is that it's an extremely binary way to make a living. You're either making a sale or you're not. Make every effort to be "on" during every moment you actually communicate with potential customers. Take nothing for granted, and don't get bogged down with overpreparation. Do it.

I realize, of course, that research has its place. But you should never forget that if you don't make the calls, your efforts are going to be in vain. Selling is selling: going after people and talking to them. Don't lose sight of that, and don't let your obsession be misdirected into something that won't help you put numbers on the board.

Three crucial ideas—obsession, implementation, and utilization. How do you make sure you're incorporating them? Here are some tips.

Make a to-do list. Identify important objectives before you start the day; then work like crazy to attain the objectives on your list.

Keep your motivation up. This book is an excellent start; you might also eventually turn to motivational tapes or seminars. Whatever your approach, make a commitment to find one new idea a month and run with it.

Start early. Try coming into the office forty-five minutes before everyone else does. You'll be amazed at what you can accomplish, and how big a jump you'll get on your day. Don't think of it as an inconvenience—think of it as an advantage. And just do it.

Be obsessive, but disciplined. Utilize everything you have at your fingertips; then implement. It's a proven recipe for success. Remember: obsession is essential ... but obsession without discipline equals chaos!

Strategy #2

Listen

Perhaps the easiest way to distinguish successful salespeople from unsuccessful ones is to watch how they interact with a prospect. Do they do all the talking, never letting the prospect get a word in edgewise? If so, it's a good bet you're looking at a failure.

You must let the prospect speak about himself or herself; the information you'll receive as a result is invaluable. Ramrodding your points through, and merely overpowering the person rather than showing how you can help, is a sure way for you to descend into the stereotypical "hard sell" that no one likes. Such behavior is a great way to lose sales.

To be sure, you and I really believe that our product will help the person we are sitting across the table from. And yet, even though we believe that in our bones, we have to listen—not lecture. Listening is the only way to target the product to the unique set of problems and concerns the prospect presents to us. By staying focused on the objective of helping the prospect (rather than "getting" the prospect), we build trust. And trust is vitally important.

When you get right down to it, a good salesperson doesn't so much sell as help. You can pass along important information, and ask for the sale after you've demonstrated clearly how your product can help achieve an important objective—but ultimately, the prospect has to make the decision, not you. Ideally, you have to know what it will take for the prospect to do the selling himself or herself. In this environment, listening becomes very important.

Listening doesn't just mean paying attention to the words that come out of the prospect's mouth. Very little of what we actually communicate is verbal; most is nonverbal. Be sure you're "listening" in such a way that allows you every opportunity to pick up on nonverbal cues. By doing this—letting the prospect get across what's important to him or her—you'll stand out from the vast majority of other salespeople, who simply talk too much.

When your prospect wonders something aloud, give the person enough time to complete the thought. When your prospect asks you a pointed question, do your best to answer succinctly—then listen for the reaction. Allow the speaker to complete sentences—never interrupt. (What's more, you should let the prospect interrupt you at any time to get more information from you.) Express genuine interest in the things the prospect says. Keep an ear out for subtle messages and hints the prospect may be sending you.

When you do talk or make a presentation, don't drone on. Keep an eye on your prospect to make sure what you're saying is interesting. If it isn't, change gears and start asking questions about the problems the prospect faces—you are probably missing something important. Of course, you should never come across as hostile or combative to the prospect.

You probably already know that the first ten or fifteen seconds you spend with a prospect have a major impact on the way the rest of the meeting goes. This is because there is an intangible, feeling-oriented "sizing-up" phenomenon that occurs early on in any new relationship.

Much of who you are and how you are perceived as a communicator—brash or retiring, open or constricted, helpful or manipulative—will be on display in a subtle but crucial manner in the opening moments of your first meeting with someone. Make sure you are sending the messages you want to send. Before the meeting, avoid preoccupations with subjects that have nothing to do with the client; these will carry over even if they never come up in conversation.

Perhaps you're wondering: "What if the conversation is going nowhere? How do I listen if there's nothing to listen to? Shouldn't I start talking about what makes my company great? Shouldn't I get in there and make a pitch?"

Probably not. The odds are that early on in the meeting you simply do not know enough about your prospect yet to go into a long presentation. So avoid doing that. Instead, focus your questions on three simple areas: the past, the present, and the future.

What kind of widget service was used in the past? What are the company's present widget needs? What does the prospect anticipate doing with regard to widgets in the future?

Add a "how" and a "why" where appropriate, and that's really all you need. Take notes on the responses you get. After you summarize the points the prospect has made, you may be ready to talk in more detail about exactly what you can do to help solve the prospect's problems. But be sure you listen first.

Strategy #3

Empathize

Put yourself in the prospect's shoes—you'll understand how to sell to the person better.

An empathizing attitude is a far cry from what most salespeople feel about their customers. The typical comment I hear on the matter goes something like this: "Frankly, it doesn't matter to me why the guy bought what he bought. He bought it. And I got the commission." Does that sound to you like the way to build repeat sales?

Certainly, it is crucial to put the right numbers up on the board. But that's exactly why you must always make sure you're making every effort to see things from the prospect's point of view.

Sometimes salespeople forget to take into consideration what is going on in the other person's head. But think about your own experiences. Did you ever walk into a room where a person was angry, but you didn't know it? Maybe you wanted a coworker to give you a hand on a project you were having trouble with. So you stepped in and made your request in an offhand way, and before you knew it, the other person was barking out orders, stomping around the room, and generally making your life difficult. You probably could have gotten further with your task if you'd taken a moment to size up how the other person was feeling—and why.

Try to establish what is going on in the prospect's life on a given day: what feelings are likely to surface? For example, if you are dealing with someone whose company is going through a merger, you can make a guess that the prospect may well be concerned about losing his or her job. Perhaps this is not the person who should be subjected to your most aggressive approach. Perhaps things should go a little more slowly.

Just as important, bear in mind that the prospect you are talking to is going to be doing something that many businesspeople try to avoid: talking to a salesperson. It's a little naive to assume that your first visit with someone is going to be eagerly anticipated. In all likelihood, the person has probably managed to set aside a few minutes for you out of a very busy day. Treat the prospect with respect, and realize that you are probably not the most important thing that's going to happen to him or her that day.

How do you find out about the person you are talking to, so you can empathize? The best way, of course, is to ask appropriate questions and carefully monitor what comes back to you in response. More importantly, make an effort to be sincere. Sincerity is often the last thing people expect from a salesperson.

Do you really care about the people who you talk to? If you don't, this attitude will show through. One salesperson I worked with some years ago simply could not sell to anyone younger than about forty-five. The reason? Deep down, he really didn't respect his younger prospects. They picked up on that—even though the meetings were always cordial—and his sales suffered as a result.

Exhibit genuine concern about the person and his or her problems, and ask questions that demonstrate your care. React properly to those questions. Above all, keep your conversations straightforward and sincere—avoid peppering the person with probing questions right off the bat, and don't let your interest sound fake or forced.

This may be difficult at first. Maybe you have been bruised one time too many, or become a little jaded in your sales career. Maybe you have forgotten the fun of the business, lost sight of the thrill of making a sale as a result of a good, solid, honest initial contact. If so, you must make every effort to relearn the enthusiasm and sincerity that builds trust. That effort will pay off handsomely for you.

Strategy #4

Don't See the Prospect as an Adversary

They have a saying in the advertising world: "The customer is not stupid; the customer is your spouse." I suppose you could adjust it somewhat for sales: "The prospect is not an enemy; the prospect is your fiancé."

The prospect should be your friend. Always strive to get the two of you working together.

I'd like to have a dollar for every time a salesperson has talked to me about that so-and-so down the street who just welched on a deal. Or for every time I heard about someone coming on so strong that the prospect slammed down the phone receiver, or—worse still—threw the salesperson out of the office during a scheduled meeting.

I've never had a prospect of mine become an adversary, and you shouldn't either. There's simply no excuse for letting your sales work result in a large number of enemies, rather than a long list of allies.

Don't fall prey to the ridiculous advice you may hear about how you have to beat up on a prospect before he or she beats up on you. This approach is rude, arrogant, antisocial, and unprofessional. But those aren't the most important reasons not to follow that advice. You shouldn't beat up on the prospect for one simple reason: doing so loses sales.

The prospect would rather be your friend. Just as you want the prospect to like you and give you business, the prospect really would prefer to be your friend. Many salespeople find this hard to believe, but it's true. Most of the situations in which the prospect seems to cut things short have to do with either a hectic work environment or an unprofessional approach by the salesperson.

The degree to which the potential for goodwill is retained is based on how well you do your job. See your prospect as someone you want to do business with; an associate, someone you can talk to while you both work to attain goals.

The best selling arises from win-win situations. That means you win because the prospect wins. You are not out to "get the order now" if doing so is not going to help your prospect. When the prospect buys something from you, he or she is buying a benefit. That benefit (faster production, lower operating costs, higher sales, whatever) is what you must keep your eye on. Not your sales totals.

If you see your prospect as an adversary, someone you are going to outwit, outsmart, or show up, you are never going to be successful. You are, instead, going to lose that potential customer, and probably build up a bad reputation in the process.

Let me tell you a story that illustrates what I mean. Karen was a sales rep who had just started out with a major business machine company with an office in Manhattan. Karen did not yet understand that she wouldn't get anywhere by treating the prospect as an adversary. This led to some major errors in strategy on one sales call in particular. How major? Read on.

Karen had scheduled an appointment with an important prospect, one she'd been phoning for weeks. She showed up at the scheduled time, only to hear at the reception desk that her contact had had to deal with some unexpected problems, and would need to reschedule.

There are any number of ways to deal with that situation. What Karen did, however, is a textbook example of how not to deal with it.

Karen made such a fuss at the front desk that her contact actually had to drop what he was doing and make his way out to the reception area to try to explain what had happened. The contact asked politely if Karen could call tomorrow to set up another appointment. Karen refused. She'd waited long enough, she said. She had to meet with the contact now, today. After about five minutes of this, the contact gave up and started to walk back to his office. Karen tried to follow him.

Exasperated, the contact turned on her and ordered her out of the building. Did that faze Karen? Of course not. She figured she could outwit this guy any day. Karen said to him, "This is too much. I can feel the tension getting to me. If you don't spend the time with me that we agreed to, I am going to have a seizure right here." Her objective: embarrass the guy into sitting down and talking to her.

Isn't that a wonderful way to build up a professional relationship?

It got even worse. The contact said, "I won't do it. Get out of here." Karen then actually fell down on the floor and faked a seizure. Two gentlemen from building security had to come and escort her out of the building. Would it surprise you to learn that she didn't get the order?

Perhaps you're laughing at that story. But ask yourself how many times have you approached it the same way? Do you ever curse under your breath in the middle of a tough cold call? Do you ever persist in calling people who obviously have no use for your product or service? Do you ever walk into a sales appointment fantasizing about how you're going to "nail" a prospect? If you can overcome these habits—and it may take work—you'll distinguish yourself from a lot of bitter, nasty salespeople out there who can't understand why people don't want to talk to them.

We once ordered some copiers for our office. We'd had two bids; the sales rep that lost called and asked why we bought the other machine. I explained in detail why I had made the decision I did. The salesperson didn't agree with my decision, though, and began to yell at me. Didn't I know that the machine had a 90-day warranty, free this and free that, half-off such-and-such, and advanced thingamajigs at no extra charge? How on earth could I make such a mistake? What was wrong with me?

Needless to say, that exchange didn't change anything. Well, I take that back. It did change something. It made me absolutely secure in my original decision. Obviously, this was not a customer-oriented organization I was dealing with. And I made a mental note never to have anything to do with the Confrontational Copier Company the next time I needed to expand my office copier pool.

Your goal as a salesperson is to create mutual trust. You simply can't do that in an adversarial environment. Be patient. Make repeat visits when necessary. Always listen to what the other person has to say, and accept your prospect's goals as your own. Most important, don't fixate on closing the sale so much that you lose sight of your prospect's dignity.

Strategy #5

Don't Get Distracted

By giving the prospect all your attention, you will, in turn, win the prospect's undivided attention.

Recently, a young salesperson came to my office on an appointment. He went through a rather lengthy discourse about his product; I sat in silence.

He came to a point where he had apparently been instructed to ask his prospect a few questions. He asked them dutifully, but somewhat stiffly, as though he were reciting a speech. Time after time, as I began to answer him, I noticed that the salesperson was staring off into space, paying no attention whatsoever to what I was saying. He might as well have been on a coffee break. Perhaps he wished he were.

Many salespeople are so busy running down their checklist of things to do that they forget they're dealing with another human being, and start focusing on things that have nothing to do with the sale.

Part of the reason for that has to do with the stress associated with selling for a living. Often, when confronted with a stressful situation, we'll seal ourselves into a comfortable little world of our own—a world that we can usually control, but that carries with it the very real risk of missing something important.

It's estimated that the average salesperson actually sells for less than 5-½ hours a week. In other words, if you're like most salespeople, you're not selling every single hour of every single day. You're doing other things: getting ready to see prospects, making your prospecting calls, writing up proposals, attending meetings, filling out paperwork, and so on. That's why it's so vitally important to make every minute you actually spend with a prospect count. Accordingly, you must concentrate on what's being said; don't daydream or get sidetracked.

When you get distracted during a sales call, you distract your prospect. You begin to fidget; you wonder what's for lunch; you think about the movie you're going to tonight; you let your mind wander when it shouldn't be wandering. This throws off the whole meeting, because your prospect will sense what's happening, and will wonder what's wrong. The atmosphere of trust won't materialize—and that's bad news. You need that trust.

If you need an incentive, remind yourself that, directly or indirectly, the prospect is telling you the single most important thing you will hear all day: whether he or she will buy your product, and why.

Take notes to help you concentrate. Make sure your briefcase is well organized, with everything you need at your fingertips. The tools you bring with you to the meeting should help you, not stand in your way. If you find yourself spending five minutes fishing a brochure out of your valise, something's wrong.

The same idea applies to the common problem of attaching too much importance to a confusing or negative remark from the prospect. If the prospect tells you left is right and right is left, don't get befuddled, don't demand an explanation, and by all means don't challenge the person. What will you gain? Ask politely for a clarification if one seems in order, then settle back and pick up from where you left off.

Try to get a bead on the prospect's interests and personality. Ask your basic questions. Then repeat the prospect's ideas. ("So what I'm hearing is that your chief concerns are . . ..")

Where appropriate, let the prospect take the lead, and pay attention to what happens next. By isolating factors unique to this particular prospect, you'll remind yourself that you're dealing with another person—one who's important enough to give close attention.

Strategy #6

Take Notes

Note-taking is an essential part of the rapport-building and information-gathering process, and it is an enduring mystery to me why so many people fail to use this basic sales strategy.

Assume that I've already worked through the prospecting stage by reaching you through a cold call. Let's say I'm coming to your office now on a sales appointment. You and I meet. We shake hands. You tell me to sit down. I do. You look at me; I look at you. We exchange a little small talk, find out a little bit about one another, and establish some commonality. As the meeting progresses in this way, there will come a moment when you look at me and say, in one form or another, those words that so many salespeople have come to dread.

"Well—what can I do for you?"

That's the point where the real work begins. How I handle that first transition can make or break my sales call. Fortunately, I have a notepad and a pen. And those tools are going to help me establish a solid, professional relationship with you.

In response, I say to you, "Well, Ms. Jones, I work for ABC Widgets. We happen to be the largest manufacturer of widgets on the East Coast, and we've worked with about fifteen companies in your industry, including JJ Resources. And the reason I wanted to talk to you today was to find out if there was anything we could do to work together to increase your production. Actually, I had a couple of questions I wanted to ask you about that. Is that all right?"

And I take out my pad and pen. Automatically, I've made a statement. Just by doing that much, I've shown you that I'm professional; I'm organized; I'm in control; and, most important, I'm concerned about your interests (increasing production).

You say, "Sure, go ahead."

And I proceed to ask you about the past, the present, and the future, with regard to your use of widgets.

Note that I don't respond to your "what-can-I-do-for-you" line by talking about how wonderful my Model X Widget is. I can't do that yet, I don't know enough about you. I have to learn more about what it is you need—and get you to talk about yourself and your company—by asking questions and taking notes.

Anyone who uses this technique for any amount of time will find that prospects talk more when you have a pen and pad out than they will if you just ask them the question point-blank and skip taking notes. Your note taking reinforces the prospect's desire to speak, and this, of course, gives you more to write. It's a self-perpetuating cycle.

The Many Benefits of Taking Notes

Among the many advantages of taking notes during an initial meeting with a prospect are the following:

1. Taking notes makes you focus on solutions. Note-taking will reinforce, both for you and the prospect, the reason you showed up in the first place; to learn more about the prospect's problem.

2. It helps you listen. There is something about having an empty sheet of paper in front of you that really tunes you in to what is being said, and it makes it more difficult for you to miss important points.

3. It puts you in a position of authority and control. Believe me, during the opening twenty minutes or so of most first-time sales visits, you can use all the help on this score that you can possibly get. By the same token, however, adopting the "interviewer" position by taking notes allows you to put your contact, simultaneously, into the position of the expert and, in a strange way, allows him or her to secure an even higher status in the relationship. It sounds contradictory, but once you try it, you will see how taking notes elevates the status of the person you are talking to as well as your own status.

4. It strengthens your analytical abilities. If you write down notes during your interview, you are using three senses: touch (that is your hand which is doing the writing), hearing (what you have to do is listen to the prospect) and sight (to see what you have written). My experience has been that by approaching a problem through all three of these means of sensory connection, you are usually in a much better position to come up with a solution.

Taking notes will also encourage the prospect to open up. You may doubt this, but try it first. Every single time I conduct a seminar, I get further proof of how effective the simple act of writing something down (in this case, on an easel) can be in encouraging communication. When I simply stand in front of an audience and ask, "What was good about the presentation we just heard?"—nothing happens. When I stand in front of an easel and write "GOOD POINTS FROM PRESENTATION" across the top then ask for suggestions—wham! The room comes alive!

Taking notes sends strong positive signals to the prospect, and you can never do that too much. When the prospect says, "I have 500 trucks, each of which holds seventy-five widgets, making deliveries 320 days a year," and then looks over and sees that you have written "500 x 75 widgets x 320 days/yr," guess what? You have scored! You care! You are really listening!

Some Suggestions for How to Do It

I suggest you use a standard yellow legal pad with a hard cardboard backing. It needs to be stiff enough for you to be able to write on while it is on your lap. Keep your notes clean and spare; use up plenty of pages. Stay away from the backs of envelopes or unwieldy pad/portfolio sets; these will detract from the professional image you're trying to present.

Remember that your notes should be legible to both you and the prospect at all times. Wherever appropriate, draw oversized diagrams in your notes that will help you emphasize a point you are making verbally—always make a point of showing your diagrams to the prospect, and discussing them. Do not use this as an excuse to monopolize the meeting, but do use it as a means of taking what you have learned and using visual displays to show how you could add value to the prospect's organizations.

Try it. You'll find it works like nothing else on earth. Make your prospect feel as important as a movie star giving an interview, or a political candidate holding a press conference. Then use the information you gather to target your approach as you advance to the later stages of the sale.

Strategy #7

Follow Up

When was the last time you wrote a thank-you letter after your first meeting with a prospect?

Many salespeople ignore this crucial step. By taking the time to write a simple, personalized note on company stationery, you help the prospect to remember you—and you put your future sales efforts on a stronger footing.

A friend of mine is a bass fisherman; he told me about a little trick he uses that seems to me to be applicable to sales work. It's pretty simple. When fishing for bass, you must keep the line taut once you get a nibble—otherwise the fish will lose contact with your line and swim away.

A neat, courteous, and professional follow-up letter keeps your line taut—even if it's inappropriate to start reeling in your "fish" right away. Your brief typed note serves as a tactful, professional reminder of your visit, and can reinforce the positive points of your visit.

It can be as simple as, "Dear Jill: Just wanted you to know what a pleasure it was to get to see your plant firsthand. I'll be dropping by with that proposal we discussed on Wednesday as scheduled. I'm quite certain we can work together to increase your widget production. Sincerely, Peter Salesperson."

Why bother? Well, after your initial meeting—even if it went well—you have to ask yourself an important question: What do you think happens in the prospect's mind when you walk out the door?

Do you really imagine that the prospect continues to think about your product, and about how sharp your presentation was, day in and day out? Do you suppose the prospect comes in to work the morning after your visit and thinks, "Gee—how long do I have to wait until I can meet up again with that salesperson I saw yesterday?"

Many salespeople seem to act on this assumption—though what's really likely to happen, even after a spectacular visit with a request for another appointment, is that the prospect will stop a couple of days after your meeting for about three tenths of a second and think, "Now, what's scheduled Wednesday? Oh, yeah—the widget guy. Gotta keep that open."

And that's if you're lucky.

You must keep your line taut—keep your contact fresh—by making the minimal investment of time and care necessary to assemble a short thank-you letter. And, once we accept that, it's simple logic to send follow-up letters at later crucial points of the sale as well—after a major proposal, for instance, and, of course, after the decision to do business with your company.

At the later stages of the sale, you may move on to handwritten notes, perhaps including interesting clippings from relevant industry publications. Early on, however, you may run the risk of appearing overfamiliar or pretentious by using these techniques. If in doubt, stick with a good printer and sharp company stationery. (Note that it is unnecessary and often excessive to shower a prospect with "little somethings"—a dozen golf balls, say, if you learn the person likes golf.)

Of course, it doesn't hurt to drop your current customers a line now and again, either. I don't know why so many salespeople assume

23

that once a prospect decides to do business with you, no further encouragement is necessary to make that prospect a lifelong customer. Don't make that mistake. Invest five minutes, an envelope and a stamp, and make a lasting positive impression.

Treating current and prospective customers like professionals worthy of respect is always good business—and follow-up letters are just the tools you need to do that.

Strategy #8

Keep in Contact with Past Clients

This ties in neatly with #7, of course, where we talked about keeping in touch with prospects and current customers by mail. The operative idea here is that someone who decides to use your product or service, then falls out of your current customer base, is probably still a highly qualified lead. That person deserves your attention; keep in touch.

Help clients to keep you in mind. Especially if a significant amount of time has passed (and that may be anywhere from a few months to several years), past clients will often come to a point where they need your product or service again, but don't remember how to get back in touch with you!

When a salesperson calls you for the first time and passes on his or her contact information, do you instantly enter that information to your address book? Probably not. It is usually incumbent upon salespeople to remind potential customers—tactfully and professionally—that the salesperson's company is still out there delivering excellent results. Don't pester people to death, but do give past clients all the facts they need to work with you again.

It's been estimated that you have a one-in-two chance to get business from an existing account, and a one-in-four chance to get business from an old account. When you're prospecting for new customers, the odds drop to one-in-twenty. Without diminishing for a minute the importance of getting new customers, you can see that keeping in contact with your old clients really does represent significant revenue for you.

Keep an organized file of inactive accounts; call or write key people at these companies on a periodic basis. Don't do this in an intrusive or unprofessional way—just keep in touch, as one professional to another.

This approach needn't be an intrusive "hard sell," nor must it proceed at the rapid tempo many salespeople bring to their prospecting work. After all, you already have a relationship with the person. Stay calm, stay friendly, and stay professional. Don't rush things. If the person isn't in a position to buy right now, check back in a month or two.

Strategy #9

Plan the Day Efficiently

You must be absolutely dedicated to getting the very most out of your day, and planning ahead on a daily basis is part of that.

Let's face it: Committing to a daily schedule is of paramount importance. Your success or failure in this area will have a major impact on your overall performance as a salesperson.

There are a lot of time management books out there. Unfortunately, most of them are so complicated, and take so long to read (let alone implement) that they're virtually worthless for most of today's salespeople. In this section, we'll examine a few brief ideas you can incorporate into your daily routine instantly—so you can start seeing results with the beginning of business tomorrow. To start with:

- Don't waste hours planning your time when you could be speaking with clients. Plan your day the evening before.
- Prioritize your goals. Don't just start filling out a schedule willy-nilly one evening; make a list of all the things you want to accomplish, then rank them in the order of their importance before you include them on your schedule.
- Leave time for crises. Scheduling every day to the brim will cause you to slip from your plan. We all know that strange, unpredictable problems

have a way of cropping up from time to time. Leave an hour or so open at the end of the day to manage sudden difficulties. If no crisis arises, you can always move on to your next priority item.

- Get up fifteen minutes earlier than you do now—and give yourself a positive charge of energy in the extra time. Starting the day in a rush gets things off to a bad start. Begin the day with a positive affirmation: "This is going to be a great day." Eat a good breakfast. Listen to pleasant music. Stay away from reading or listening to the news first thing in the morning; it's too depressing. Be nice to yourself. (Don't worry, it won't last long.)

- Buy and use a doctor's appointment book—the kind with the whole day marked off in fifteen-minute increments. Then keep close watch on the time you spend on any given item. This approach will help you avoid the temptation to allocate vast chunks of your day to vaguely defined goals when you assemble your to-do list.

You should also buy a second, smaller book—one that can fit in your pocket or purse. Here you will record what you actually do during the day. Nothing extravagant, just a quick jot-down of the time for each project you undertake as you work through the day. The beauty of this is that you end up with a written record of events, not just your plans, and you can compare the two at day's end. If there's a huge discrepancy between what you plan at 6 P.M. on Tuesday and what you've actually done by 6 P.M. on Wednesday, you'll know about it and be able to work on it. If you're like most salespeople, you'll probably realize in doing this just how much time you spend on the road. Chances are that you'll acquire a new enthusiasm for scheduling quality appointments. You'll also have hard evidence of your own habits—lunch at a certain time, so many calls in the morning, so much downtime between meetings, etc. By knowing these "givens," your daily planning will become much more effective.

On Friday evening, prepare not only your Monday morning schedule, but also your thumbnail sketch of the week to come. Odds are that this will take the form primarily of meetings and other commitments; don't feel you have to account for every minute of every one of the next five days. Just block out your scheduled appointments and meetings so you have a good solid overview of what's on the horizon. Where appropriate, leave yourself "into-and-out-of" time. After all, you know that you won't simply materialize out of thin air at your three o'clock appointment across town, but will have to drive there, leaving early enough to assure arrival ten minutes or so before three.

By attending to daily scheduling matters conscientiously, and comparing your actual results with your plan, you'll increase your time-effectiveness and lay solid foundations for your sales success.

Strategy #10

Look Your Best

Some years back, I worked for a successful Broadway publicist and promoter who had an interesting habit.

Every day, after lunch with a client, he would come back to the office and, before going into his next appointment he'd step into the restroom, spruce himself up, and change his shirt. He'd tackle the second half of the day looking just as polished and confident as he had at 8:15 that morning.

Now, I'm not suggesting you go out and expand your work wardrobe by a factor of two. It's the mindset I want you to look at. After all, if you're like me, you've probably seen plenty of sales-people wander through an afternoon with crooked ties, mussed-up hair, and the spaghetti sauce from lunch emblazoned on their chests.

If you're a prospect, you remember someone who walks in the door looking sharp. Such a salesperson makes an instant positive impression, and has already done a lot to win respect and trust in those crucial first seconds. So check yourself out in the restroom before each and every sales appointment. You might even carry a compact mirror with you for those times you can't reach the facilities. Look sharp.

A salesperson I know started out at his new job looking just that way—sharp. But as the months went by, and as he became a little more familiar with the routine, he started coming in wearing his "B" shirts now and then. You know what a "B" shirt (or blouse or skirt) is: a little frayed, a little worn, a bit threadbare at the edges, but good enough to get by with if people don't look too close.

Your prospect will be looking close.

Don't let the fact that you do what you do every day fool you into thinking that your prospect deals with the same repetition. Each prospect you encounter is an exciting new opportunity, and should be treated as such. You wouldn't walk into a job interview wearing a "B" shirt; don't walk into a sales call showing anything less than your best.

When it comes to work, stay away from any piece of clothing that doesn't instantly communicate your status as an intelligent, organized professional. Save the casual wear for the off hours. Keep in mind that, for a salesperson who meets people regularly, who lives or dies by first impressions, there are certain things that simply have to look impeccable: fingernails, hair, shoes, clothing.

Failing to look sharp just leaves an opening for the next salesperson who does. Don't give up that competitive edge. Show the world your best side, every day.

Strategy #11

Keep Sales Tools Organized

Your professional image, as we've seen, depends to a large degree on your personal appearance. However, you should also keep in mind that it depends on your tools as well.

What do you suppose goes through the mind of a prospect who, upon meeting a salesperson, sees all sorts of objects tumble randomly from his or her opened briefcase?

Your briefcase should give the impression of order and precision when opened. It should not be overflowing with laundry lists, last week's newspapers, dirty ties, bills, or food.

It should contain your legal pad, your business cards, your pens, appropriate product materials and/or samples, a handheld calculator, and perhaps your pocket-sized datebook. That's it.

Often, salespeople will bring too much to an appointment. You don't need everything in the building to talk to a single prospect, and even though carting along reams of samples and brochures may make you feel more secure on the way to the appointment, you're likely to look confused and befuddled as you paw through it all trying to find the material you want.

Obviously, if your type of selling demands a display of a tangible product, you'll need to incorporate that element, perhaps with a smart-looking sample case. But stay away from the fancy flipcharts, display boxes, and framed testimonials. They're virtually always more trouble than they're worth. Usually, the only thing you can count on from all this extraneous materials is a less confident, poised presentation.

If you find that you're going to your appointments so weighed down with samples and display cases that you're exhausted from the minute you walk in the door, you will eventually have to make a change somewhere. If it's agony for you to carry all that, it will be agony for the prospect to look at you. Try to pinpoint the prospect's areas of concern. You can always bring requested material on your second visit.

As we will learn a little later in this book, business can be compared, in many respects, to war. Both require strategy, planning, competition, intelligence, and so forth. If you think of your sales work in that way, you'll see that your sales tools are really part of your ammunition. As such, they should be maintained with care and respect.

Strategy #12

Take the Prospect's Point of View

Get to know your product or service thoroughly, isolating how it helps people. Only in this way can you apply your knowledge to the prospect's needs.

Salespeople usually know that they should outline product features: those constant, intrinsic elements the item presents. Someone selling a tin can might call attention to the fact that it's curved along the edges, and that it holds a certain amount of material. A fountain pen, in the same manner, can be said to have a point, or to write with ink. This book might be described as being rectangular, or written in English.

All true. And all very boring.

Features are essential—no one wants to buy a fountain pen that does not have a point—but features are not usually the first thing on the prospect's mind. Typically, the prospect will be concerned with a different idea entirely: benefit. And this, too, must be emphasized by the salesperson.

Benefits are what the user will get out of an item. A tin can, when considered by a food-processing firm, might be said to have a benefit if its design allows more cans of soup to be produced in a given day than the design of a competing can. And someone comparing this book to another book on sales might notice that it's broken into 101 brief, easy-to-read chapters—an important factor for a salesperson who's pressed for time.

What about your product or service? What benefits can you isolate? What tangible advantages do your customers have over the customers of the competition?

Once you begin to see things from this perspective—the potential customer's perspective—you'll be able to start assembling the key selling points of your product or service. It is a common mistake to concentrate instead on features, and subject the prospect to a barrage of confusing technical information of limited interest.

Think about how you approach buying something. Your main concern is not how the lawn mower, refrigerator, or automobile was assembled in the first place, but rather how the whole conglomerate will help you mow your lawn, get ice when you need it, or achieve good gas mileage.

If the salesperson focuses on those goals of yours, he or she will be speaking your language—and will be able to communicate essential facts about the product.

If, on the other hand, the salesperson starts talking about rigid-comb titanium construction with DL-X latex-bearing modules, you're going to smile, nod politely, and pretend you understand what's being said. Unfortunately, though, you won't be any closer to knowing what you want to know about the product.

You should, if possible, use the product or service as a customer. Research your product or service thoroughly from the prospect's point of view; isolate benefits. Then you'll be able to make crystal clear the advantages your prospect will have by choosing you.

Strategy #13

Take Pride in Your Work

Some years back, I went to do a program at a major consumer products company. During a question-and-answer period, I asked the participants to call out the reasons their company should be considered number one in its field.

I stood there in front of the flipchart, marker in hand, waiting. No response. After a little while, a hand went up. "Yes?" I asked. "You know, Steve," the man said (and I'm paraphrasing him here), "we may be number one on raxilated widgets, but when it comes to looking at world midsized widget production, I think we actually rank around number four."

"No," a woman called out from the back of the room. "No, six. Midsized widgets, we just got the new rankings, we're sixth."

"Sixth," said the man.

Another pause.

"Okay, well that's interesting to know," I said. "Anything else? What is there that really makes this company great? Anyone?"

A man in the front row cleared his throat.

"Yes?"

"The new cafeteria," he said slowly, "is certainly nice."

Just then, a younger fellow asked to be recognized.

"Yes?" I said. "What is it about this company that really gets you going?"

He looked surprised. "What?" he asked. "Oh, no, I just wanted to say something. Mort mentioned the cafeteria. They've had some plumbing problems, I just thought I'd let everyone know it's out of commission this week."

"Then I take back," said Mort, "what I said about the cafeteria."

"You know what bugs me," said a young lady on my right, "is the way they changed the pay schedules around. We used to get reviews annually, on January first. Now they're doing it by your anniversary date with the company, which means I'll get a raise six weeks later this year."

You see my point. The group I was addressing had not taken it as an article of faith that one should take pride in one's organization. Instead, when asked to list positive aspects of their work environment, they either put forward petty complaints or said nothing at all.

That's not the way to make your company number one, and that's not the way to make yourself number one, either.

If you can't stand behind what you do and where you do it with every fiber of your being, why bother? Why punch a clock? Why show up in the morning? Why do something that, clearly, you do not enjoy doing? Why ask people to buy your product or service if you don't believe in it?

If you don't take pride in your product or service, and in the organization that stands behind it, you will not be successful. If you focus only on the negatives, the obstacles, the reasons you can't sell the way you should—guess what? You won't sell the way you should.

Pinpoint factors that mark you as superior to your competition. Become comfortable discussing those factors in an optimistic way. In short, talk your organization up. Don't just do this at work, though it's certainly essential there, but mention where you work and why it's great at parties, social gatherings, conventions—everywhere. (By the way, this will not only build your optimism about the business, but also expose you to a whole new universe of potential customers.)

Suppose you have a real problem with your company. Suppose the reason you don't feel great about where you work goes beyond normal sales cycles or standard management headaches, and is instead rooted in some legitimate, deep-seated objection. For instance: you have a moral problem selling what you sell. Or the quotas you must meet are so high that the whole staff burns out on a regular basis, and turnover is always high.

Does any of that mean you shouldn't be enthusiastic about where you work?

No. It means you should be enthusiastic about where you work, but you should work somewhere else.

If you can't get behind the program 100 percent, find somewhere you can—then give it everything you've got. Be proud of where you work, and what you do for a living. You'll see that good results will soon follow.

Strategy #14

Beware of Trying Too Hard to "Convince"

When you really want to make a sale—I mean, desperately want to make a sale—it's easy to slip into a "convincing" mode. You'll corner the prospect, you'll review why your product or service is great, you'll get past all the troublesome objections, and finally the prospect will see the light of day and buy from you.

The only problem is, it's exactly the opposite of what you have to do. You have to commit to understanding the problems and concerns of the prospect, not steamrolling over them. And you have to work from there to demonstrate in a compelling way how your product or service can address the relevant concerns.

In short, you have to convey value and benefit, rather than convince the prospect that his or her concerns are unfounded. Remember: It's always better to let the prospect do the talking, and act on the concerns he or she expresses, than to do all the talking yourself and expect a yes answer.

I know it's important for you to make sales. That's the whole idea behind the work I do, and behind every word of this book. But most successful salespeople come to realize that being too anxious to close a sale, and working like crazy to get the prospect to see your point of view, are only going to decrease your odds of closing.

Sales is not about getting other people to see your point of view. It's about getting you to see things from other people's points of view.

If you are committed to helping your prospect solve a problem, "convincing" is irrelevant. The issue is not changing someone's mind, but conveying to the person exactly why and how you can help solve a pressing problem. And you have to see and understand that problem before you can hope to solve it.

Think of how you felt the last time you had something "rammed down your throat" by a high-pressure salesperson. Did it make you feel better about the company the salesperson worked for? Did it make you want to go back again for another purchase? Did it make you want to recommend the company to others?

The important question is this: Are you interested in developing a sales career, or are you interested in developing one sale?

When people have been overwhelmed by a salesperson, when they feel doubts about the wisdom of a purchase decision, when they're afraid they may have been cheated, they say, "Some salesperson sold me this." When people really feel good about a product, they say, "I bought this." That's the difference between a one-time sale and a good solid customer. Which would you rather have?

Convey, don't convince. That means:

- Build trust and rapport.
- Find out what they do.
- Emphasize relevant past successes.
- Highlight credible solutions to important problems.

Strategy #15

Never Underestimate the Prospect's Intelligence

It's not uncommon to hear a salesperson say something like, "You know, the prospect I met with today was so dumb—he had no idea what I was talking about." Maybe you've even heard yourself making remarks like that.

My question to you is this: What does that say about you as a salesperson?

You are a conveyor of information. You are a conduit. You are the connecting unit between your business and the end user.

How can a prospect know the ins and outs of your business before you explain anything? And why, for that matter, should that prospect need to know more about your business than your phone number, anyway?

There is one area, though, that the prospect has a great deal of knowledge about—knowledge you need. And that area is his or her problems. Remember, solving customer problems is what sales is all about, and you will—or should—spend a great deal of time trying to ferret out information from your prospects.

Considering all that effort, it doesn't really make sense to proceed on the assumption that the prospect doesn't know anything. Clearly the prospect does know something important; otherwise you wouldn't set up meetings to try to learn that something.

Your job is to learn the problems the prospect is having, and then show how your product or service can be used to competitive advantage in solving those problems. You must approach this task as the prospect's partner and as an equal. If you bring arrogance or a superior attitude to the appointment, your sales will suffer.

The prospect doesn't know your product or service as well as you do because he or she doesn't sell it for a living. You do, and you should be able to provide essential information immediately, not shake your head in disappointment that the prospect isn't catching on as quickly as you'd like.

You can encourage the efficient flow of information between yourself and your prospect by being scrupulously honest with the prospect about your company and what it has to offer. Acting otherwise can cause big problems. I was working with a company that produces industrial machinery recently. One of their sales reps was indignant that her prospects had "lied" to her about the status of forthcoming orders. As it happened, this rep's whole approach to customers was flip, glib, and, on the whole, disrespectful. My guess is that she herself was not completely honest in dealing with her prospects. Is it any wonder she got bad information back from them?

As long as you and your prospect, working together, can define the problem to a degree sufficient for you to be of help, the prospect is quite intelligent enough. Your goal is not to dwell on what you consider to be the prospect's shortcomings, but rather to encourage an extremely intelligent decision: that of doing business with your firm.

Strategy #16

Keep Up to Date

Knowledge is power. Suppose you walked in to see a current customer on an appointment, and your contact had lost an arm since you'd last seen him. Would you notice?

Granted, something that obvious probably wouldn't get past you. However, there are clues and tip-offs that are, from the point of view of the prospect's business, just as blunt—clues that are visible from the moment you walk in the door, but that many salespeople miss.

What is going on in the businesses of your clients? Do you know? If there were a major layoff in the offing, would you hear about it? Is the business doing well? Is a merger in the works? Are key people happy with your product or service, or is it something a budget-cutter might consider expendable?

Too many salespeople tend to think of "closed sales" as static things, and very little in business is static. The sad truth is, no business exists for the sole purpose of purchasing your product or service. If your customers do well, you will do well—and, conversely, if they do poorly, you will do poorly. Whatever the case, it is to your advantage to have accurate information ahead of time.

Observing the prospect closely, making an effort to understand exactly what's happening at his or her business (and why), will help you gain a broader outlook on the whole environment in which your company operates.

Of course, watching your prospects firsthand isn't the only weapon at your disposal. There are innumerable reports, journals, and newsletters available to you—and if you have many clients in a given industry, it's a good idea to keep up with that industry's trade news.

A salesperson I know named Marcia had been trying to get in touch with someone at a large company regarding her company's courier service. She was getting nowhere, and when her contact asked her to "send along some information," she was convinced that she'd reached a dead end. Still, she dutifully mailed the information, but nothing happened for weeks. She wrote the account off.

Six months later, she received a call from her contact at the firm. Could she come in for an appointment right away? She could, and did, and she made a big sale. Curiosity got the better of her, though, and at the end of the meeting she came right out and asked: Why had they waited so long to respond? The answer: The company's main competitor had begun a new program earlier that year that required courier service. They were getting in on it now, and wished they had known about what their rivals were up to earlier.

The moral, of course, is that had Marcia been able to keep up with industry publications and/or gossip, she might well have been able to tell her contact how a courier service was working out for others in the industry—and closed the account months earlier.

Who does your prospect sell to? Who are your prospect's competitors? How do these competitors sell? What are the main differences between the products and prices of your prospect's firm and its competitors? What is the prospect's market share? What is the prospect's perceived market share? How does your prospect plan to deal with new obstacles? New opportunities? Are any new technological breakthroughs on the horizon? How do all these factors affect decisions about whether to buy from you?

Avoid needlessly complex and drawn-out research, but keep your eyes and ears open, and read essential publications. The more you know, the better off you'll be.

Strategy #17

Know the Four Steps of a Sale

No matter what you sell or where you sell it, your sale can typically be broken down into the following stages: *qualifying, interviewing, presentation,* and *closing.*

Let's examine each stage individually.

- Opening/Qualifying—Also called prospecting or cold calling, this is where you contact someone you've never spoken to before (often by calling them on the phone) and determining that there is a possible use for your product or service. You may set up an appointment or future call date at this stage.
- Interviewing—You learn the past, present, and future with regard to the prospect's use of your product or service. You find out what special problems have presented themselves recently. You learn other pertinent facts about the prospect.
- Presentation—You show exactly how your product or service can help solve the problems identified during the interview stage. You appeal to past successes with other customers.
- Closing—You ask for the sale.

It's possible that you can proceed through all four stages in a single telephone call. It's also possible that it will take you months or even years of appointments and follow-up appointments to go from making your cold call to reaching and completing the final stage. All that depends on the product or service you offer, your industry, its customers, the prevailing economic conditions—a number of different factors.

At any given point in the cycle, your objective is to move from where you are to the next stage. In other words, if you are qualifying, your goal is to move on to interviewing; if you are interviewing, you want to get to a point where the prospect is comfortable with a presentation, and so on. There is one rule, though, that you must bear in mind in considering the cycles I've outlined above: The simplest and most reliable way to lose a sale is to move from one stage to the next before the prospect is ready to do so.

Many salespeople view their work as one gigantic closing stage. By failing to understand the cyclical nature of their work with a prospect, they rush things and lose sales.

Let's say you have a garden. One morning you walk out into your garden and sow seeds for a tomato plant. If you're a smart gardener, you'll realize that it's going to take most of the summer for the tomato to make it from the seed stage into your salad bowl. If you wait a couple of weeks, see something vaguely tomato-like emerge from the ground, rip it up, and smother it with vinaigrette dressing, it's not going to make for a very good (or even edible) salad.

If, however, you give it time and let it mature, it will blossom into a juicy, ripe tomato. Then you can brag about it. But if you rush the process, you're not going to get anything for your efforts.

Selling is the same. There are certain things for which you simply must wait; otherwise you're not in the sales business, you're in the rejection business. You're a professional collector of rejections.

You should not attempt to walk into an office for the first time, shake hands with a prospect, and ask when the operations department would like to receive the first order. In this instance, you are attempting to rush from the interview stage into the closing stage, and your results will be disastrous. Most problems of rushing, however, are not that obvious. Perhaps you've talked a little bit about yourself, mentioned your product, admired the view, gotten a little past history, and received an assurance that what you're talking about "sounds interesting."

Are you ready to move on to the presentation stage? Maybe—and maybe not. The best option is usually to ask the prospect straight out: "Well, is there anything else you think I should know about your company, Mr. Smith?" Depending on the answer you get, you'll be able to gauge the prospect's enthusiasm for moving on to the next stage. When in doubt, err on the side of patience. There's no crime in saying, "Well, I've learned a lot about your company today; what I'd like to do now is set up an appointment for next week so I can go over a completed proposal with you."

Strategy #18

Use People Proof

What is "people proof?" It goes something like this: "Mr. Jones, I know this program will work for you, and I'll tell you why. We had a company in your industry, ABC Tires, that was very skeptical about what we said we could do for them. But they did try the program, and we did in fact deliver the results. And I know that the same thing can happen here with your firm."

That's "people proof," and it's some of the most powerful ammunition at your disposal. People proof reinforces positive inclinations toward your company, and gives people a logical reason to confirm the emotional decision to do business with you. If you can cite another business (or, better still, another business in the same industry) that's had success with the product or service you're offering now, you're well on the way toward building the trust and confidence necessary to close the sale.

Many salespeople react badly when I make this suggestion. They say, "Steve, it won't work for me; I work in an industry where confidentiality is important."

I've got news for you. Everyone works in an industry where confidentiality is important.

It's a simple enough matter to clear such informal use of client names ahead of time. After all, you're not giving away company secrets—just disclosing the fact that you worked for a certain firm. You do the same thing when you type up a client list.

Just mention to your contact at ABC Tires that you'd like to be able to include his company (and perhaps even his name, if he's agreeable) in your literature and personal presentations. Keep the atmosphere casual and friendly; don't make it appear that your customer is making any kind of commitment to you. You may be surprised at the results. The normal customer reaction is to be flattered, not paranoid.

People proof works wonders. It makes you less of an untested quantity, and more of a proven problem-solver. It builds legitimacy in the eyes of the prospect, and helps you get down to the important business of solving problems through your product or service.

Strategy #19

Act Like an Equal—
Because You Are One

You are a professional. There's no need for you to abase yourself or fawn over a prospect rather than work with the person to solve a problem. Doing so usually has a negative—rather than positive—effect on your sales efforts.

At a program I was conducting a while back, I made a recommendation to a salesperson named Myra that she not only try to meet with her contact at a certain company, but also attempt to set up a meeting with the head of the firm. She was shocked at this suggestion.

"Oh, Steve," she said. "I can't do that."

"Why not?" I asked.

"Well," she explained, "if I ask my contact to put me in touch with the president, the answer might be no. Then where would I be with my contact?"

There's a new idea, don't you think? A salesperson being confronted with the word "no"—certainly a unique event in the daily life of a salesperson, and certainly an excellent reason not to try something in the first place.

Myra, I learned, was not with the company three months later. Why not? Well, think about it. That exchange she and I had said a lot about the way she looked at her contact—and at sales as a profession. She was petrified at the idea of offending her contact, and my guess is that it was because she believed deep down that the contact was doing her a favor by giving her business.

In short, she relinquished control of her sales environment, and humbled herself to contacts. Her thinking probably ran something like this: If I'm nice enough to Mrs. Jones, if I take her out to lunch every week, if I remember her kids' names and birthdates, if I never give her a reason to have a free, open, give-and-take discussion with me—if I can do all that, maybe, just maybe, I'll get on her good side enough for her to buy a widget from me.

Something's missing there, don't you think?

Where does Mrs. Jones's company's need for widgets come in? And where does Myra's role as conduit and facilitator come in?

My guess is that Myra could not see herself as a professional—as a partner. Instead, the Myras of this world tend to see themselves as supplicants.

Are you a professional? Or are you still in the process of trying to gain professional respect from your prospects? The paradox is that the very act of trying too hard to gain that respect will turn people off to what you have to say.

How you look at yourself, of course, has a great deal to do with how others look at you. This is why a commitment to ongoing motivational work is so terribly important.

No one's saying sales is easy. No one's saying you'll never get rejected and no one's saying there won't be days where, despite all your best efforts, you feel like you're simply not getting anything accomplished.

Nevertheless, you must find an internal reservoir of strength, confidence, and security in your identity as a professional, and you must convey all that to your prospect—as an equal. Because that's what you are.

You must operate from the assumption that you bring to the table a specific set of skills and a level of product knowledge that the other person can benefit from. If you operate on the opposite assumption, that the person across the table from you has a prize that you can win if only you can prove yourself worthy to him or her, you're in trouble. The only people you're going to win over (if you're lucky) are extremely insecure prospects—and those people are not the ones who tend to achieve the highest levels of success in business.

When you stop to think about it, my bet is that you'll see that the people you'll most want to work with (and emulate) have a strong sense of self, of confidence, and of professionalism—and have every expectation of the same from you.

Don't let them down.

Strategy #20

Don't Get Fooled by "Sure Things"

There's a saying in baseball about never taking your eye off the ball. The same advice applies to salespeople who get so excited about a big sale they think is all but sewed up that they stop prospecting altogether.

There's nothing wrong with a little healthy enthusiasm, but when you spend hours (or days) dreaming about how you're going to spend the money you'll pick up from the Kilgore deal, watch out. Those dreams are costing you money, because they're nibbling away at time you should be spending developing new customers. Those dreams are letting you justify being complacent; and complacency is something a good salesperson can't afford, no matter how good things on the horizon look.

Daydreams on the job are troubling enough, but what's even more disturbing is when salespeople make a big deal out of potential sales that really aren't that promising. We move here beyond simple complacency and into outright self-deception. I'd like to be able to say here that such problems are rare, but unfortunately they're all too common.

And it's not that difficult to see why. Salespeople thrive on hope. When you've been turned down all day long, it's very tempting to treat the first nibble you get as The Big One You've Been Waiting For. However, you can gain some vitally important perspective by thinking a little bit more deeply about your sales cycle.

What I'm about to outline is something that can, for some people, turn an entire sales career around. For others, it will take years of misplaced efforts and untold frustration to realize fully the implications of the seven simple words I'm about to pass along.

You make money when someone says "no."

How is that possible? How on earth can you expect to make money by hearing a prospect tell you he's not interested?

Easy.

Let's say you make twenty contact calls a day. Of the twenty decision-makers you reach, not everyone is going to want to make an appointment with you. You don't walk to your desk, pick up the phone, and expect twenty appointments from twenty calls out of yourself. You're smarter than that.

You expect, say, five appointments. Of those five appointments, you can expect to close perhaps one sale. (These ratios can vary from industry to industry and from salesperson to salesperson, but you get the idea.)

Let's say that you get a $200 commission on that sale. Now, most salespeople tend to think of all the work that went into that sale—the calling, the appointments, and so on—as some sort of administrative hassle that it would be nice to be able to avoid. They see the work that precedes the sale as a technicality, and spend all their efforts trying to zoom in on that one big call that simply equals $200.

But that's not really the way it works, is it? In fact, you do have to make those twenty calls in order to have the five appointments that lead you to the sale. And, when you think about it, if you cut those calls in half, and only make ten every day instead of twenty, you'll be cutting your sales in half, won't you?

In short, every call you make, and every appointment you go on, is part of your personal sales cycle—including the rejections!

You could even look at it this way: For every contact call you make, you "earn" $10, even if the contact says, "No thank you, we're already using ABC Widgets because my brother-in-law works there and he gives them to me for free, so please don't ever call again."

Now, with this perspective, you can see that having one big sale, while certainly nice, isn't going to do you much good in terms of your long-term overall cycle—because you're going to want new sales next month, and the month after that. And you can also see that, if the Big One doesn't come through, that's disappointing, but really no problem if you put adequate effort in on both ends of the cycle—the twenty calls and the one close. There will be other Big Ones waiting for you down the line.

Keep your eye on the ball—and don't get fooled by "sure things."

Strategy #21

Don't Take Rejection Personally

Having discussed in the previous chapter how you make money when someone says "no," we're in a good position to look more closely at the whole issue of rejection and how salespeople react to it.

For a salesperson, as we've seen, a rejection is not a personal affront, but rather part of the overall cycle inherent in any day's work.

Salespeople simply must learn to look at the issue in this way. After all, there's only one surefire way to avoid rejection—and it works like a charm. That way is never to ask for anything. Don't ask for the appointment; don't ask for the sale; don't try to show your prospect how you can help solve problems. You'll never get rejected. Unfortunately, you'll never make any money, either.

One man I worked with recently, Frank, was trying to make the transition from work as an administrator to a job as a field sales representative. He went into the new position with high hopes. After all, he was a people person. He loved talking about his product. And he knew it inside and out.

However, he was not prepared for the amount of work he had to do to make his efforts worthwhile. He learned in short order that, to get to a realistic number of "yes" answers, he had to be willing to listen to a lot of "no" answers. And that was tough for him.

Frank had worked for fifteen years in a totally different environment. He had grown used to working for weeks on a proposal, having that proposal passed around and returned to him with suggestions, and then putting together another draft—a draft everyone believed in.

Now he was asking himself to move from that slow, consensus-oriented job to a rapid-fire, binary, on-or-off world that profoundly confused him.

He said to me, "Steve, it's not a matter of my not knowing that rejection is part of the cycle. I know how many people I have to see to make money; that's how many people I see. And I'm doing all right. But I'm completely stressed out. When people turn down my product, it feels like they're really turning me down. And that's hard for me to adjust to at this point. I wish I could change the way I look at things; I know I've tried."

Ultimately, Frank decided that sales wasn't for him; and looking back on it, I'd have to agree with him.

I'm not telling you this story to convince you that if you don't like rejection, you should get out of sales. Nobody likes rejection, and it's natural to feel some disappointment when you hear someone say "no."

But the crucial issue is how you deal with that rejection. If you can teach yourself to accept that the fact that the person says "no" is not a reflection on you, your product, or your company, but merely in the course of things, you can dust yourself off and move on to the next prospect.

But if, over time, it's impossible for you to teach yourself that, then a career in sales is going to be very difficult for you. There's a good chance you'll even start to take out the stress you feel on prospects that have no intention of rejecting you. If that happens with any regularity, there is very little chance for you to succeed.

Unfortunately, not everyone is cut out for a career in sales. Some people, like Frank, simply have so much invested in other work modes that a change really isn't a realistic option. For others, fortunately, it's possible to pick up the resilience and self-assurance necessary to approach the issue of rejection from a detached, professional point of view.

Whether you realize it now, the main obstacle in approaching the issue of rejection is not how the prospect thinks of you, but how you think of yourself. Don't be too hard on yourself; accept steady progress happily. If you can eventually make the necessary adjustments, and not take rejection personally, you'll be on your way to sales success.

Strategy #22

Understand the Importance
of Prospecting

As you've probably gathered by this point, I place a tremendous
amount of importance on the act of prospecting for new customers.
There's a good reason for this. A solid commitment to prospecting
is the one habit that, if developed correctly, is most likely to ensure
sales success.

You can have problems keeping up with technical advance-
ments. You can stumble occasionally during in-person presentations. But if you prospect effectively, you can compensate for these
problems—and be quite successful in spite of them.

Part of the problem is that salespeople tend to look at prospecting
in general (and cold calling in particular) as a chore to be avoided.
As we've seen, avoiding the prospecting stage is senseless; prospecting is the first, crucial stage in the development of new customers.

"But," you may be saying to yourself, "I don't need new customers. I just closed six accounts. I'm going to get repeat business from
them. I'm all set."

Wrong.

You may think you're all set for now, but you are not all set for next month, or the month after that, or next year. Even if things do look great right now.

We all know that sales is an up-and-down endeavor. There are good months and bad months. It's the nature of the beast. Many of the "downs" salespeople experience, however, are preventable. These slumps often result, not from seasonal dips in business or economic decline on a large scale, but from the failure of salespeople to make sure that they have prospects in the pipeline at all times.

A friend of mine who was working for a large insurance company was doing extremely well. One year he took in nearly $200,000 in commissions, and established himself as the star of the staff. One day, though, he called me. His voice was tense, and I could tell something was the matter.

"Steve," he said, "I'm in trouble. I wasn't prospecting."

Star of the staff or no star of the staff, my friend had dug himself into a hole. He'd gotten cocky. He'd made a lot of money, but he'd spent most of it on fancy vacations and expensive toys. He'd neglected his prospect base for the better part of a year, had developed no new clients, and was now watching his income drop precipitously month by month. He was working like crazy just to make up lost ground.

You're never so successful that you can ignore prospecting. You never have a base of clients that's big enough to last forever.

Most salespeople are well advised to make a certain number of cold calls every day, no matter what. I recommend talking to twenty decision-makers. Whatever number you settle on, make prospecting part of your routine; block it off in your schedule.

Keep something in the pipeline all the time; you'll regret it if you don't.

For more information on prospecting skills, see my book *Cold Calling Techniques (That Really Work!).*

Strategy #23

Never Focus on the Negatives

I've worked with many salespeople, and I've come to the conclusion that there are some people who simply spend their whole careers inventing and/or reinforcing obstacles.

Everyone's seen this in action: the water-cooler gripe sessions, the behind-the-back gossiping, the snide remarks on off days. The potential topics are innumerable. Office politics. Perceived defects in the product or service. Impossibly tough competition. Endless personal problems. Unfair commission schedules.

As that noted sales trainer Roseanne Roseannadanna might have put it, it's always something.

Now don't get me wrong. We all have problems, every single day. But some people enter the ring half-beaten, and some enter considering the battle half won. A successful salesperson must fall into the latter category; a persistently negative outlook will not only make it difficult for coworkers and supervisors to work with you—it will make it difficult for prospects to work with you.

It's common for me to hear a salesperson complain, "Steve, you don't understand how much is expected of us here." My feeling is that most of the time this is nothing more than a martyr act on the part of the salesperson. I've met with hundreds upon hundreds of sales managers, and their goals are usually pretty clear-cut: Get good results from the staff. Not necessarily walking-on-water results, but at least keeping-your-head-above-water results. (It's interesting to note that most of the people who complain about how high their quotas are complain only during dry spells; if business is good, the same quota can be considered quite manageable.)

If you're not making sales, complaining about everything in sight is only going to compound your problem. Not only will you be wasting valuable time you could be using to talk to new prospects, but you'll also lose perspective you need to identify and resolve the problems you're having.

Many companies have had the experience of having a salesperson perform poorly in a certain territory, complaining that "the market is saturated" within it. Take that person off the territory, put someone else on it, and—shazam!—sales take off, saturation or no saturation. The difference? Usually, the first salesperson fixates on limitations, while the new rep brings no preconceptions to the work, and sees fresh opportunities as a result.

Selling is difficult work; no one is saying it isn't. But you must be able to isolate problems, deal with them, and then get down to business. Remember, your workplace is where you must work toward making sales. Doing anything else—specifically, letting yourself get caught up in negative diversions—is simply giving away your competitive edge.

Stay positive. Stay upbeat. You are your own greatest asset; focusing on negatives keeps you from performing at your peak.

Strategy #24

Get Competitive

The writer Henry J. Kaiser may have put it best: "Live daringly, boldly, fearlessly. Taste the relish to be found in competition—in having put forth the best within you."

It's almost impossible, in my experience, to succeed at a high level in sales without nurturing and celebrating a competitive spirit. Ultimately, having a competitive spirit means being willing to do anything and everything you possibly can to exceed your own highest standards.

How do you develop a competitive spirit in the world of sales? There are any number of ways. Here are a few to consider.

Keep an ear open for intelligence about your business rivals. You talk to customers all day long; find out what your competition is doing, and, just as important, what they're saying about you. Pass key facts on to your "commanding officer."

Report problems immediately to superiors. If you learn of a customer problem with your product or service that seems serious enough to warrant some rethinking, don't keep this to yourself. Tell the "brass" so something can be done immediately.

Develop a team mentality. Realize that others in your company—administrative people, production people, others in the sales department—are all working toward the same goal you are: success for the firm. Avoid pointless conflicts with coworkers. Share crucial information that will help your company surge ahead. Emphasize positive, optimistic thinking at work.

Set goals and then go all out to attain them. Consider your daily schedule to be a battle plan, then give your every effort over to the goals you establish. Do not allow complacency or acceptance of mediocrity to take root. And when you notice your company's rivals in the marketplace starting to gain on you, take comfort in the words of Gil Atkinson: "Thank God for competition. When our competitors upset our plans or outdo our designs, they open infinite possibilities of our own work to us."

Strategy #25

Communicate That You Are a Person to Be Trusted

I have trained more than 500,000 salespeople. And the more salespeople I run into, the more exposure I get to various "tricks of the trade"—little corners salespeople cut in order to get ahead (or so they think) over the short term. The only problem is, too many of these "tricks of the trade" undercut an essential objective: that of consistently sending and reinforcing the message that it is a good business decision to trust you.

The "Raffle" Trick

I know a car dealer who uses such a "trick" to get people to come into his showroom. He opens up the White Pages, finds a name, calls the person, and says, "Hi, Mr. Jones, this is Mike Johnson at Johnson Used Cars. You've just won our raffle! Come on in and collect a turkey!" What he never says is that he really wants the person to come in and collect two turkeys: one to put in the oven and the other for the driveway. (By the way, there is no raffle; the turkeys are bought as premiums for anyone who walks through the door.)

The same salesperson would call up someone at random and claim to have found his wallet, "just to get his attention," then launch into his pitch. How much would you trust an approach like that?

I am not trying to be harsh toward those who sell automobiles for a living. Some of the most effective salespeople I know sell used cars. But I am trying to say something about this used car salesman. By starting off with "Hey, you've won a free turkey," he was using a cheap trick. It seems to me that it was no coincidence that he sold cars to match. Word gets around about that sort of thing.

If you sell turkeys, talk about turkeys. If you sell cars, talk about cars. Talk about exactly why it makes perfect sense to buy the one you have to offer. Beware of the tricks of the trade. If they come at the expense of your credibility, they are too expensive.

"Follow Me!"

The successful salesperson makes a good leader because he or she inspires trust. I think that the truly successful salespeople today—and, by the way, this is what I see in the world-class sales forces—have the personal magnetism and the self-assurance to say to people, "Follow me"—and thereby win long-term, happy customers. That kind of authority only comes with complete, unflinching confidence that you can deliver results for your prospect. If you are right about that, you communicate the message that it is sound business to trust you—and your customers follow you.

Too many salespeople focus on whether or not they have learned to appear trustworthy. That is not the point! You want to develop an earned reputation for following through on everything—and I mean every syllable—that comes out of your mouth. If you think such "minor details" do not have any real persuasive power, I have to disagree with you. At the beginning of your relationship with a prospect, those details are all he or she has to go on. They are the only tool you have! Spout lavish promises and fail to follow through on the details, and you will be like every other salesperson. But say you are ready, within the next five minutes, to fax over a quote that completely meets all the prospect's specifications, and then do it . . . and you are one in a million.

Relationships are built on trust, and trust is built on evidence of all kinds. This does not mean that you must show you are subservient—that is the opposite of being a leader! You must demonstrate that you are unfailingly dependable in all things, big and small, and you must make a habit of delivering what you promised (or, preferably, more). Then you will be in a position to say with authority, "Follow me."

Strategy #26

Take the Lead

Be sure to tell the prospect where you are at any given point in the sales cycle. Do not be afraid to steer the conversation in the direction you want it to go.

Here is what it might sound like:

> "Well, now that we have come this far, Mr. Prospect, I will tell you what I would like to do. I would like to take these notes and go back to my office and talk to some of our people there. Then I would like to work up an outline of how we might be able to work together and come back here and show that to you next Tuesday at 2 o'clock. Would that work for you?"

How many sales are sabotaged by salespeople who want to avoid "offending" the prospect, and somehow never get around to mentioning what they want to happen next in the relationship? Take charge. Make a conscious choice to inform the prospect with regard to where you both are in the process. The alternative is long, "good" meetings that end in that odd, results-free limbo that leaves neither party sure what to do next.

We do not live in a perfect world. We live in a world of complex people who have complex thinking patterns—people whose next action may not be obvious to us. It follows, then, that we run the risk of having the prospect stop us and say, "Hold on—wait a minute. I am not ready for that yet. You are moving too fast for me."

So what? You need that information. You need to know where there is still a problem to be worked on. If you do not know where there is a problem, you will not be able to close the sale. And it is far better to isolate a problem through a consistent system of "sequence updates" (as I like to call them) than to wait until the last minute, ask for the business, and then find out there was something important you should have been paying attention to but were not.

Getting the information you will need to move ahead in the sales cycle is important—even if it means hearing something you would rather not hear right now.

Sometimes, as a result of these updates and the feedback you receive from them, you will isolate important issues or potential obstacles to the sale. You may find that, even though you went in the door thinking about selling Widget A, and even though the prospect seems interested enough in Widget A, the questions that keep coming up as you try to move the process along seem to concern the applications you know could only be obtained through Widget B! Your objective is to solve problems—not to make the prospects fit your preconceptions! So you move on to Widget B. But you can only do this because you have listened to the feedback your updates have yielded.

Let us be clear on one thing: Sales cycles will vary from industry to industry and from customer to customer. What that means in plain English is that you never know when someone is going to agree to buy something. I am not suggesting that you try to manhandle the prospect. Even if you issue the update I am talking about, you still have to be willing to work with the prospect, every step of the way. And you can't do that unless you both know where you are and where you are going.

Strategy #27

Engage the Prospect

Engaging the prospect is a special undertaking. It is difficult to define. I might start out by telling you what it is not. Engaging the prospect is not reacting instantaneously, as if by reflex, to every comment or perceived disapproval.

Every prospect is different. Every prospect reacts differently to what you have to say. Some seem to have all the time in the world, while others consider a fifteen-minute meeting to be a major crisis in time management. Some have made careers out of being skeptical, and others pride themselves on free thinking, even outrageous approaches to problems. Before this, you cannot earn the respect of all of them with a single "script" designed to "handle the first few minutes." You must identify what is important to any given prospect, and then learn how to appeal to those values.

Here are some general suggestions on drawing out your prospect and initiating meaningful conversations. Of course, you will have to adapt them to fit particular situations.

First, discuss that with which you are familiar and comfortable. Avoid venturing opinions on Abstract Expressionism if you know nothing about that branch of modern art; do offer your insights on topics that you share an interest in with the prospect. Your confidence in the subject you select—and connect somehow to the other person—will carry over. There is an advantage to beginning an exchange by focusing on your own observations and experiences—concisely and tactfully, of course. Doing so takes some of the pressure off of your prospect, who will be expecting you to try to "draw him in." Just be sure not to overwhelm the person.

When the person starts to talk about himself, "lean in" to the conversation. Remember it is virtually always a good idea to get the prospect discussing his or her own experiences. I like to do so by asking, "How does a person get to be a . . ."

Show that you care by really caring. Remember, you are there to help. When the prospect outlines a problem, show the same concern you would show if it were yours. After all, you want it to be yours!

Strategy #28

Know Why Your Company's No. 1
Account Bought from You

Do you know why your company's top customer bought from you?

If you don't, you should.

You should know, and be able to discuss, exactly how much that deal is worth, what led that account to closure, and what's on the horizon in your company's relationship with that customer. You should know when the company decided to buy. You should know what they decided to buy. And you should know who made the decision.

This is mandatory whether you closed the deal yourself, or whether a colleague closed the deal.

The contacts at your prospect companies will be interested in these facts. So master them! Pick up the phone right now and call whomever you have to call in the organization to figure out why your largest account (the account that now generates X thousand dollars a year) decided to buy.

You should then share as many details as you can of this sales success story during meetings with prospects. (Make sure that you do not violate the confidentiality requirements of your top customer.) The story will break the ice and give you credibility.

Once you've mastered the details of your company's number-one account, get the details behind as many of your "top" clients or customers as you possibly can.

Sometimes salespeople assume that the only success stories they can or should share with prospects are those they had some direct role in bringing about. In other words, they imagine that if they didn't personally close the deal, they have no "right" to offer the details behind a customer's decision to use their company's service. What a mistake! The minute you walk in the door, you already have the right to share every success story your company ever generated! Be sure you take full advantage of that right.

When we train new salespeople for our sales training organization, you can bet we don't make them wait a month or two, in order to close a deal personally, before they start talking about the benefits we've delivered to clients like Aetna, Boise Office Solutions, LexisNexis, Clcarnet, and Sprint. We clear the details of those stories with our clients, give them to our people, and make absolutely sure that they know them and are comfortable discussing them at a moment's notice!

Strategy #29

Handle the Leads That "Fall into Your Lap" with Care

It's a dream come true. You are on the job, minding your own business, when suddenly someone calls, seemingly out of the blue, and virtually asks you for business. Wow!

I know what the first temptation is. You want to close the sale. Life is tough enough; you spend all day building, establishing, persuading. Now along comes The Sale You Deserve and you are sure as heck not going to let it slip through your fingers. So you start to move in.

Don't.

It will take some discipline. Let us be honest: It will take a lot of discipline. But if you really want to move the lead from the other end of the receiver to your commission check, I promise you that the surest way to do it is to take a deep breath, count to three, and follow a few simple steps.

1. Back off and establish some kind of relationship. If this really is someone you have never spoken to before, you do not know whether a brisk let's-get-right-down-to-business, of-course-we-can-solve-your-problem

approach is going to work. It may backfire spectacularly, and often has. So exchange a few pleasantries; get a feeling for the kind of person you are talking to.

2.   Find out what is going on. Say, "I am really glad you got in touch with me; listen, do you mind if I ask what prompted your call?" This is very important! You have no idea exactly what you are dealing with yet; no sale exists in a vacuum. Things may not be what they seem! Sometimes people call, sound like they are going to sign on with you, but really need generous amounts of tender loving care. Establish your surroundings; get the information. Do not succumb to the temptation to sell—it may be too early.

3.   Ask to set up an in-person appointment or otherwise secure a slot on the person's calendar for some point within the next two weeks. Yes, you should do this even if the person tries to close the sale himself on the phone. (Unless, of course, you are involved in telemarketing.)

You need to establish a personal bond, and you need to get the person to invest more time and energy into the relationship.

Do not assume you have a "sure thing." The truth of the matter is, these types of calls do not always turn into revenue. For one thing, people may simply be shopping around to a number of different vendors. Move the relationship forward, and try to get face to face. If you do so, your efforts will pay off handsomely.

Strategy #30

Know How to Make Your Product or Service Fit Someplace Else

How can you adapt an existing product or service to satisfy a new situation? In my seminars, I talk about product/service "malleability." The word means "flexibility" or "capacity of being adapted."

Dentists use gold and silver for fillings because of the malleability of those metals. They are easily manipulated, and provide a complete, secure fit over and within a cavity. Along the same lines, you might want to think about the ways your product or service can be adjusted or customized for new prospects in order to help you meet specific requirements and goals.

Let's take a look at a simple example. Suppose you are in the paper clip business. How many ways do you think you could use paper clips? Obviously, you can think of a paper clip as a small metal item used to fasten sheets of paper together. But if you stop and think about it for a moment, you will realize that people use paper clips for all kinds of different purposes. Some people twist them into makeshift cotter pins; some people use them to clean out hard-to-reach places on office equipment; some people use them to fix eyeglasses; some people make decorative chains out of them. I personally have used two paper clips as a tiny clamp to extract a stubborn disc that would not eject from my computer's drive.

There are probably a hundred different uses for a paper clip besides holding sheets of paper together. Are there a hundred different uses for your product or service that you may not have considered before? Before you dismiss the possibility, keep in mind that you do not need a hundred to boost your sales. You need just one good idea.

Baking soda is for cooking, right? Well, it can be. But for some strange reason the Arm & Hammer people made a big deal about running those ads promoting its use as a refrigerator deodorizer. By the way, do you know anyone who uses baking soda that way now? My bet is that they did not before the people at Arm & Hammer started that ad campaign.

Ask yourself:

Does what you sell work in only one way? Or can you adjust it? Can you make it serve some new purpose or function? Can you present it in a different light or to a different group of people? The key lies in opening your own mind to new possibilities, then following through.

Successful salespeople work with their prospects and customers to develop creative new answers to the questions "What do you do?" and "How can we help you do it better?"

A story I tell during training programs shows how that final question can develop naturally during the interview phase. A few years ago, a museum was unable to get its insurance for precious works of art to kick in during a critical period of time—the period after paintings on loan had arrived at the museum's central facility but before the assessor could inspect and catalogue them.

A sales rep for an instant camera company made a multiple-unit sale to the facility, but she didn't do it by asking "Why don't you use instant cameras in your operations?" Nobody at the museum had thought about using instant cameras, so she wouldn't have gotten a constructive response by asking a question like that. She found out during an interview about the objective of a particular decision-maker to make those dangerous three- to four-day lags between arrival and insurance coverage go away. Then, based on her thoughtful, open-minded discussions with her contact, she made a proposal. "Based on what you've told me here today, it sounds like you might be able to use a couple of our instant cameras to catalogue your recent arrivals. You could overnight the photos and logs to your insurance carrier, save their representative a trip, and get your coverage in place within forty-eight hours. That's what a lot of the other museums we've worked with have found makes sense."

It worked! But it wouldn't have if the rep hadn't found out what the museums did before launching into a preprogrammed spiel. The same goes for you. The more you find out about each and every area of a prospect's business that has some possible connection to what they do, the more likely they are to find a new selling possibility.

Successful salespeople never stop asking:

- What does the person do?
- When does he or she do it?
- Why does he or she do it that way?
- How can I help him or her do it better?
- How does he or she do it?
- Where does he or she do it?

And they never stop thinking of ways they can turn the answers to those questions into new applications and solutions.

Strategy #31

Pretend That You Are a Consultant—Because You Are

Treat all your sales work as a consulting assignment. Many years ago, I found myself hopelessly stuck while working for a new prospect. I was trying to develop a program for him and things simply were not working out. So here is what I did. I said, "Charlie, rather than go any further with this, let me think about what we talked about here and then come back next week with a couple of ideas. Then, if you like them, we can continue our discussion." He agreed to that; I eventually closed the sale.

It was shortly after that meeting that I realized what I had done. I had taken the same approach I would normally take with a client who is simply asking for an evaluation of the problems on his firm's sales desk. I had taken the "sell" sign down for a moment and come to grips with the fact that since I did not yet have an adequate assessment of the prospect's problems, I could not offer him a solution.

There is a catch to selling from the mindset of the consultant. You have to be willing to stop and think once in a while.

The best salespeople are professional problem solvers. If you sell cars, you should consider yourself in the business of solving transportation problems. If you sell copiers, then you should consider yourself in the business of solving photocopying problems. If you sell cellular phones, then you should consider yourself in the business of solving communication problems. But you have to know and understand the problem first before you can try to solve it. You have to be willing to walk in the door without any preconceived notions as to how best to solve the problems you have identified.

For many salespeople, the consultant principle can be put on an even simpler footing. If you sell to other companies, you should consider yourself in the business of solving profitability problems. That is the key concern you will ultimately be addressing: how to increase profitability. Everything you do, every proposal you offer, should lead eventually to the goal of your client's firm increasing its level of profitability. Weigh your goals and your approaches against this standard and you will have gone a long way toward achieving sales success.

If you are not interested in helping people solve problems, then I am going to respectfully suggest that you are not in the right business. If you cannot break everything you do down into something that helps another person reach an important goal, you will either base your sales on manipulating others, or fail to persuade prospects that you are offering anything of value. Either path leads inexorably to burnout and/or constant rejection. You definitely do not need that.

The dictionary defines "consult" as "to seek advice, information, or guidance from." To me, this definition encapsulates exactly the relationship between a qualified prospect and a professional salesperson. You as a salesperson are there to advise the prospect as to the ways you can help solve existing problems. You are there to provide all the necessary information relative to solving those problems.

Act like a consultant . . . because that's what you really are!

Strategy #32

Ask for the Next Appointment While You Are on the First Visit

This is one of the easiest pieces of advice to follow in this entire book. Yet it is also a step that the majority of salespeople routinely ignore. Many are even afraid to take it, even though they know it has done wonders for others!

A young salesperson once actually said to me, "Steve, that's not my place. I'm in the prospect's office. He's showing me a courtesy by seeing me in the first place. If I'm going to go back there for a second visit, the prospect should ask me."

Baloney!

You initiated the contact in the first place. You have made it clear at every point in the process that your objective is to help the prospect. You have demonstrated that you are interested primarily in solving new problems for him. Why on earth shouldn't you ask the prospect for the next appointment so you can show how you would implement the solution!

You did not set the initial appointment for your health. You did it because you had an objective: helping to solve the prospect's problem with your product or service. You still have that objective.

Therefore, it is altogether appropriate for you to ask to move the process along to the next stage before the meeting adjourns.

Unless you receive a firm unequivocal "no" during the first meeting—and even then you can ask whether or not you made a mistake of some kind—there will always be a next stage to talk about. And the best possible time to set the appointment for discussing that stage is while you are face to face with the prospect. You both have your calendars within reach. You both have pens or pencils handy. What other time would you choose to set your next meeting? What on earth would induce you to leave that room without knowing when you will next meet with this person?

"Okay, Mr. Jones; I think we've gone about as far with this as we can today. I'm excited about this and I'll tell you why. I think there's a chance that we may have a match between what you do and what we do. What I would like to do is meet with you and one of my team members to show you exactly what we can do for your company. How's Friday the 15th at 2:00?"

Listen for the response. There has to be a response of some kind! Then work from there with the information you receive.

Strategy #33

Create a New Plan
with Each New Prospect

I go through a little monologue each time I meet a new prospect. I say, "Here is someone new. Here is someone I have never met before. What am I going to do that will be a little different with this person?"

It may be routine for you, but the prospect you are dealing with has never gone through the sales cycle with you before. One of the best ways I know of to combat that "here I go again" sensation (and that is a danger for even the very best salespeople) is to produce a customized, written plan for this particular prospect. This should be based on the material you gather in your notes during the first and subsequent meetings. (See Strategy #6 for more on taking notes.)

Let's face it. After a while, you become familiar with certain objections or problems. And it is all too easy to pigeonhole your prospect. "I know that one; that is just like the problem the guy at ABC Company had." Well it is and it isn't. It is not like the ABC problem in that the person who just outlined it has nothing to do with ABC Company, and probably faces a number of different challenges related to the problem he just brought up that you know nothing about.

A prospect who offers up an objection is really making a gesture of good faith. That may sound a little bizarre, but it is true. By taking the time to share a concern or problem with you, your prospect is passing along important information, key facts on the way your product or service needs to be adapted. Listening is the first part of the secret and identifying the mutually accepted solutions is the second part. Find out what those challenges are, being sure to be aware of the unique circumstances or background your prospect may face. Then and only then should you commit the most likely solution to paper, working with your prospect, not against him or her, to determine the plan that will make the most sense in the current situation.

Look at it this way. If you go to the doctor because you have a stomachache, you do not care if he has seen 3,000 other people with stomachaches over the course of his long career. The last thing you want is for him to rush in the room, look you up and down, mumble some technical phrase you have never heard before, and scratch something on a prescription pad before hustling away again.

No. You want him to ask how you feel, how long you felt that way, whether you have ever felt that way before, exactly where it hurts, what medicines you may be allergic to, and all other pertinent questions. If a doctor does all that you are likely to be a better patient—and you will probably have a better attitude about coming to see him next time around.

Well, you are a doctor. It does not matter how many patients you have seen before; this one is the only one you are seeing now. Like the best doctors, you should make an effort to include the patient in your diagnosis and treatment. Doing so not only makes for a better atmosphere for you to conduct your work in, it also increases the likelihood your patient will have the positive attitude that is the driving force behind so many dramatic recoveries! In other words, if the person does not believe your stuff will work, you should not count on him becoming your best customer.

Strategy #34

Ask for Referrals

My favorite story about referrals has to do with a very successful salesperson I know named Bill. Every year he vacations in some exotic locale like Fiji or the Cayman Islands or Hawaii. Often these vacations come as result of company bonuses for his performance or industry awards. So about once a year, this agent sends a letter to his customers and qualified prospects announcing his return from Paradise, where he received the XYZ award for outstanding sales achievement. The purpose of the letter is to thank the salesperson's clients for their business, and to make it perfectly clear that the only way the salesperson has been able to attain his goal is by helping his customers attain theirs. Classy, yes?

At the end of the letter is the paragraph that runs something like this: "As you know, my business depends upon referrals. I would very much appreciate it if you would take a moment now to jot down the names and phone numbers of three or four people in the industry you feel might benefit from talking to me. Of course, if you do not wish me to use your name when contacting these people all you have to do is indicate this in the space I have provided below. Again, thank you for your business, and here's to continuing success for both of us."

Call me crazy. But I have a feeling there may be some cause-and-effect connection between letters like that and all those expensive vacations and impressive sales awards.

Playing the Numbers Game

Let's play a little multiplication game. Suppose five people give you five referrals each, for a total of twenty-five. And suppose that of those new referrals, 60 percent turn around and give you five referrals, too. That's fifteen times five, or seventy-five new prospects. Now if of the seventy-five, 60 percent give you five referrals each . . . you get the picture. If you are out to build your client base exponentially (and why shouldn't you be?), there is no better place to start than asking for referrals. Referrals are the lifeblood of a successful career in sales. And yet salespeople are usually terrified to ask for them.

Often, they feel it will somehow threaten the relationship they have built up with a customer to ask if there are other associates of that customer who might benefit from their product or service. Perhaps the customer really doesn't like using the product or service, after all, and asking for a referral will only intensify that feeling or bring it to the surface.

This is paranoia. If you have got a customer who is benefiting from what you do, you should find out whether he or she has people you should be talking to.

Follow your instincts.

You should be able to tell without too much difficulty whether or not you have a satisfied customer or an enthusiastic prospect. If you do, what that really means is that you have established the foundation of a productive mutually beneficial relationship. Why on earth would your customer not want to share that kind of relationship with his friends and associates?

How can you make referrals work for you? Let's say your goal is to get five new prospects for the week. Carry with you at all times a package of 3" × 5" index cards. After you are done meeting with one of your customers or a good quality prospect, simply say something like this.

"Mr. Jones, I am willing to bet there are people in your (industry, area, related business) who could benefit from my talking to them about this (product/service)."

As you say this, you take out five index cards, hold them in your hand, and let the prospect or customer see that there are five of them there. Then say, "Do you know of five people I could talk to?"

Help your contact along. It will be easier than you think; the fact that there are five separate index cards will make the task comprehensible and immediate. Your confident, professional attitude will guarantee that your request will not be seen as inappropriate.

Put the cards on a row on the desk as you fill them out, writing names only. Then, after you have identified the five referrals by name, go back and ask for the company affiliations, addresses, or other contact information. You do this because you want to make the first and most important job, identifying the people you can talk to, as easy as possible.

Taking the Direct Approach

I know of one salesperson who actually asks his contacts at this point of the meeting, "Frank, how would you feel about calling these people for me?" Of course, in some cases the contact says, "No," and says the salesperson should make the call. Then the salesperson says,

"Yeah, you're right. I probably should call them. You don't mind if I use your name, I hope?" He has never yet been turned down on the second question—which is the one he wanted a yes answer to in the first place.

Yes, that is an aggressive approach, but it illustrates the point that you can profit enormously by asking directly for referrals.

Strategy #35

Show Enthusiasm

No, this does not mean embracing your prospect, pumping hands twenty times as you shake, or issuing endless implausible compliments about dress or appearance.

There is a difference between enthusiasm and poorly disguised panic. Enthusiasm builds bridges; panic tears them down. A sales meeting is like any other interaction. It takes a certain amount of time to get off the ground. If you understand the dynamics that work when you first come into contact with a prospect, you will go a long way toward understanding how enthusiasm must be conveyed as the relationship progresses.

The Early Phase

When people meet someone new, they pass through a number of stages. There is among human beings a certain feeling-out process, and introductory stage. You cannot say convincingly at this stage all that you might want to about solving the prospects problem, because the two of you don't know each other well enough for that discussion to take place. The prospect—along with most of the rest of the adult members of our species—will require a certain "choosing" time before entering into a socialization stage with the person. So the best way to show enthusiasm in the very early part of the meeting is to underplay it. Confident bearing; good eye contact; a firm handshake, predictable, smooth movements as you walk from one point to another—these are the keys to communicating your excitement about the new relationship you are trying to build.

The Later Phase

Only you can tell when the prospect enters the second stage of socialization, but rest assured that the change will be noticeable. It will be marked by a more relaxed, open approach, often reflected in less constricted body language. What you are looking for is the point at which the prospect listens not because he has agreed to do so, but because he wants to. Once you see that shift take place—and it may be during the first visit or during the subsequent ones, you can change the "grammar" of your presentation.

You may decide to use your hands more in gesturing or to use the prospect's preferred form of address ("Mr. Powers" or "Bill") somewhat more frequently. You might even feel comfortable using less formal phrasing and word choices: "Take a look for yourself." "How about that?" "And I'll tell you what we did."

Make an effort to avoid repetitive mechanical gestures or responses. This is exactly what creates an unspontaneous, unenthusiastic meeting. If your conversational partner insisted on constantly nodding his head up and down with little real regard for what you had to say, how would you feel?

These are general guidelines; your individual interactions with prospects will vary, because prospects themselves will vary. The point is that bolstering your presentation with appropriate enthusiasm (especially on the second and subsequent visits) is an essential part of a solid sales technique.

Strategy #36

Give Yourself Appropriate Credit

Talk about yourself—but be humble. The two instructions are not mutually exclusive. I want you to learn how to do both. There is nothing wrong with walking into the prospect's office and talking with confidence and pride about what you do. Too many salespeople cannot seem to grasp that that is really the reason to show up in the first place! The only trap to watch out for is that of appearing arrogant or acting out of ignorance. Fortunately, these two traps are easy enough to avoid.

A Justified Confidence

When you walk in to meet the prospect, you will want to convey success, confidence, and flexibility.

That is not arrogance. That is professionalism, and you should be proud of it. You should be able to talk in detail about the specific success stories that made you successful.

I am not suggesting that you play "one up" with your prospect by boasting about how great your kids look, how good your golf game is, or how much money you make. That is a game you cannot win, no matter how the conversation ends.

What I am suggesting is the aggressive promotion of your ability to succeed at your chosen task, which requires a good deal of discretion on your part. You have to learn how to read the situation. You have to know when to step back. You have to know that what works for Prospect A in one situation may not work at all with Prospect B in another situation. What I am suggesting carries a very real risk that, if you do not read the signals correctly, you may overwhelm your prospect. But even that danger, with appropriate observation and awareness, is worth risking. Far too many salespeople underwhelm the prospect, and that is just as dangerous. At least with my way, you know that there is no possibility that you are going to fade into the anonymous parade of mediocre salespeople who most decision-makers have to face!

Talk Yourself Up

Yes. There is a definite risk here. But in my view it is a risk worth taking.

Try it with the next prospect you see.

"Mr. Jones, I am really glad to see you. This has been a really big week for us—we just completed the XYZ project. Let me tell you about it."

Wow! You are the person who makes things happen!

In an earlier chapter we used a doctor/patient analogy. I am going to revise it a little bit to make a different point here. This time, suppose you walk into the doctor's office and the minute the doctor walks in the door into the examining room, you notice he looks sicker than you do. He is wheezing and coughing—and holding a stubby, half-smoked cigarette between his fingers. He is tottering a little bit as he walks. His eyes are yellowish. He is having trouble focusing on things.

Is this the man who is going to solve your health problem?

For many professionals, there are two kinds of people: Those who add value to whatever they touch, and those who cause the value of everything they touch to decline. Prove that you fall into that first category. Show your value! Demonstrate it! Broadcast it! Shout it from the rooftops! As long as you do so without affecting an air of superiority, your self-promotion will be perceived as security. Not arrogance, but admirable, enthusiastic security in your own mission and your ability to carry it out.

Strategy #37

Tell the Truth (It's Easier to Remember)

Someone did a study at a university recently on the issue of exactly how many "white lies" the average person tells during the course of a day.

Do not ask me how or why someone takes it into his head to study such a thing, or how he convinces somebody else to pay for it. My question is, can you guess the results?

The answer came out to be approximately 200.

That is a lot of lying! And that is only the average. But let us be clear about what the researchers were looking for. When they went out looking for white lies, they were looking for all the times someone said to someone else, "I am glad you could come by today," when in fact maybe the person was not so glad. These kinds of false-hoods—which we could also classify as harmless social convention—are not what I am talking about when I advise you to tell the truth to your client or prospect.

Building Bridges

Salespeople are relationship-oriented. They build relationships on trust and personal contact, and they live and die on the strength of those relationships. Now, that this is the case serves as a convincing argument for telling the occasional "white social lie" and against telling any other type of lie. Let us look at a couple of examples.

"Gee, this is really a great office. I sure wish I worked in a place like this." (Actually, the office you work in easily outshines the prospect's.)

No big deal. Some salespeople find it easier to make contact with the prospect by finding something like this to comment on as they are breaking the ice. What is the problem if there is a slight exaggeration on a point like this? Even if the prospect should somehow learn the terrible truth that you work in a spectacular office, is there any real downside to such a statement made tactfully and without any overbearing flourishes? No.

Here's another one:

"And about the delivery time you are asking for, I do not think we should have any problem meeting that, though I will have to clear it with the technical people after we square away the paperwork here today." (Actually, you know full well you will miss the prospect's requested date by two weeks no matter what you say to the people in production.)

Red light! You are attempting to build a new relationship with a potential customer by deliberately misrepresenting your ability to solve his problem to his satisfaction. When things go crazy later on—and nine times out of ten in this situation, they will—the prospect is not going to remember the cute little disclaimer you slid in there about running things by the technical people. He is going to remember that you said you could deliver the product on the first and the blankety-blank thing did not make it into the warehouse until the fifteenth. At that stage you will no longer be regarded as a problem-solver. You will be regarded as a problem. A salesperson who promises more than can be delivered. This is not the stuff of which repeat sales are made.

The Slippery Slope

If you need further convincing, consider this: Once you make a habit of simply telling everyone what they want to hear, you are eventually going to run into a serious problem. You will not be able to keep your story straight. You will be dealing with fifteen different clients, each of whom has received fifteen different, customized pie-in-the-sky assurances. It will only be a matter of time until you become hopelessly muddled . . . and slip up disastrously.

Don't risk it. Tell the truth; it's easier to remember.

Strategy #38

Sell Yourself on Yourself—
Get Motivated!

The following are some ideas you can use to motivate yourself more effectively. Use them!

Do not listen to the news during your morning commute; listen to motivational tapes instead.

News broadcasts are usually filled with lots of depressing stories that you will not be able to do anything about anyway. Take the morning for yourself. Buy some motivational tapes and make a habit of making the drive (or ride) into work a time for positive messages and clearheaded sober assessments of the day ahead. I know of one salesperson so committed to this principle that he honestly does not know whether the AM/FM radio in his car works.

Be specific with your goals and your rewards.

Perhaps your dream is to own a Lamborghini—fine. Put a photo of one on your desk or on your refrigerator at home. Or perhaps you look at things a bit more analytically: Your goal is to close six new sales over the next month. Take a piece of paper and commit the goal to writing. This will make your aims more tangible and increase the likelihood that they will be attained.

Get positive reinforcement.

I think it is fascinating how many successful sales "teams" there are—two individuals who sell completely independently but who rely on each other for constant support, advice, and constructive criticism. For most of us, this really is a far better alternative than going it alone; if you can establish this relationship in your current work environment, give it a try and see what happens.

Get outside.

Yes, you do need a lunch break. No, you should not work through the noon hour. My studies on this with salespeople lead me to believe that those who make a point of putting work aside for an hour and getting outside in the sunshine are actually more productive in terms of sales volume than those eager beavers who do not know when to quit.

Leave yourself notes.

"I can do it." "Most of the things I worry about never happen." "I solve the problems for more than 500 customers." Try to leave one message like this on your desk Friday afternoon; you will probably forget about it until Monday morning, when it will be a pleasant surprise.

Keep things in perspective.

Missed calls, forgotten deadlines, problems with customers—challenging as it all can be, it is really not the end of the world. Sometimes things seem larger than they are. Try to keep that in mind as the day progresses. For me, this lesson is particularly important between about 2 P.M. and 4 P.M., as that is when my day really can start to seem like a never-ending series of brain surgery projects. Is there a similar time for you? If so, that is when you should be sure to give yourself a break.

Strategy #39

Start Early

Did you know that you can often get past the "secretary trap" by making important cold calls before 9 a.m.?

A lot of decision-makers are given to making it into the office before the rest of the crowd shows up. They might just pick up their own phone if you call them then.

That is one obvious advantage to getting an early start on the day. There are any number of others. For one thing, you will be in a much better position to handle the office-wide crisis mentality that sometimes seems to set in around 9:01. For another, you will be able to do your relaxing, newspaper shuffling, and paperwork managing at sometime other than the peak contact hours during the business day. Those are advantages that can add up in a hurry. As I am fond of pointing out, a salesperson is a lot like a retail store in that location is often the key requirement for success—only our location is the number of people we talk to during the course of the day.

There is more. My guess is you will find your commute a great deal easier if you get a little earlier start in the morning. That may seem like a minor consideration—until you realize how important attitude is in sales work. In so many of our big cities these days, you can spend an hour or an hour-and-a-half simply getting from Point

A to Point B in the morning. That is a lot of time, but the key consideration is really the aggravation you are likely to run into during that much "drive time" (or train or bus time, for that matter).

If you spend the first ninety minutes of every morning swearing at people or scowling at stoplights that seem designed to slow you down, you will probably find that your first few calls of the day are less than stellar. You will lose the hop on your fastball before you talk to a single potential customer, and that is a shame.

Time for yourself means making sure you are at your best when dealing with others.

Finally, let me add an important observation based on my experiences and those of many of the successful salespeople I have worked with: The day really does seem to go better if you can take a couple of moments of "quiet time" for yourself before charging into the fray. There is something very hard on the system about bursting through the door at 8:59 and having to hit the ground running, no matter what that entails. I have a strong feeling that salespeople who do this are costing themselves sales; the first few calls they make in the morning are "warm ups," whether they like it or not.

Of course, the best of all possible worlds would be to show up for work early enough to have a little time for oneself, and then do some role playing with a colleague to make sure the warm up calls are not directed at live prospects.

Strategy #40

Read Industry Publications (Yours and Your Clients')

Quick! What kind of people do you suppose read *American Highway Engineer?*

How about *Publishers Weekly?* What audience do you expect to subscribe to *Ad Week?* Or to *Billboard?* Or to *Variety?*

You may not find them on your local newsstand, but these publications and hundreds more like them may be the most important magazines you can get your hands on. The industry or industries you work in almost certainly have some sort of a trade journal or magazine read by just about anyone of any consequence within the field. You can put yourself at a distinct competitive advantage in comparison with many salespeople by becoming familiar with these publications. Use them to keep abreast of industry trends. You should understand and be able to adapt to the business environment faced by your customers. That means reading what they read.

Subscriptions tend to be expensive, but you can probably find back issues of the magazine or journal you are looking for in any good library, or via the Internet.

Your Winning Edge: Information

You will probably find that you can get a much better understanding of the technical jargon employed in your target group by reading the articles in trade and professional magazines. Of course, you may have some trouble with a few of the denser articles and subgroups within an industry, but you are much better off puzzling things through on paper now than nodding your head vacantly when the terms are rattled off later!

The "who's who" or "who's on the move" sections of these publications can be a particularly fertile source of sales leads. In these columns, you will find the names and company affiliations of people who have recently been promoted or hired at a given company. Who would not be flattered by a brief note of congratulations on having appeared in such a column—followed up by a phone call a few days later to talk about your company's products or service?

Keeping Track of it All

You might even decide to keep a running clip file on references to the various companies or individuals appearing in trade magazines. This can be an invaluable aid in breaking the ice when meeting with a new prospect. For my part I can tell you right now that I would much prefer being able to cite three interesting points about a prospect culled in the pages of a trade magazine than be forced to talk for twenty minutes about the weather or how attractive the prospect's kids are!

Strategy #41

Give Speeches to Business and Civic Groups

Public speaking rates as one of the most commonly shared fears human beings have. Yet I am going to suggest that you take the time to develop your skills as a speaker and get out and share your (unparalleled!) expertise in your field with your audiences—and not just audiences of people in your industry. Just about any audience, believe it or not, will do the trick.

The Expert Speaks

There is a double-edged sword at work here. First off, you will benefit tremendously from the boost in confidence you receive from being treated as an expert in your field. By the way, if you do not consider yourself an expert in your field, you should not be selling in it. Your customers are certainly counting on your expertise!

Think about it. You know your subject. You talk about it all day long. Once you can make the minor adjustment of being able to give a lecture about what you do, you will be a lecturer. Get someone to note you, and you will be a "noted lecturer." Pretty soon, there may well be a lot of people noting you. Then you will be a "widely noted lecturer." And deservedly so!

So the first benefit is reinforcement. You may know intellectually that you and your firm possess everything necessary to solve problems A, B, and C, but believe me, you will receive an extraordinary emotional charge from actually getting up onstage and talking about A, B, and C to a group of willing listeners. If you do not think that that affirmation will carry over positively into the way you deal with prospects, my guess is you have not been in sales very long.

The second benefit is even more remarkable. Studies have shown that when salespeople and consultants give speeches, an average of one out of every ten audience members will seek out the speaker afterward to ask about his or her services. What this really means is that 10 percent of any given audience you talk to will end up qualifying itself—and entering your prospect cycle! Who knows what might happen if you actually took the initiative to shake some hands and pass out business cards during intermissions and at the event's conclusion?

It may take some effort on your part to get to the point where you feel comfortable addressing a group, but I assure you the effort will be worth it. Remember that even the most accomplished professional speakers complain of stage fright. Your goal should not be to get every butterfly out of your stomach, but to learn to make the adrenaline work for you. Where to go to give the speech? Well, outside of the channels that may exist in your industry (such as addressing a trade conference, taking part in an annual convention), consider contacting your Chamber of Commerce about local round tables. Other possibilities include your area's Rotary Club, Kiwanis Club, or any group that seems relevant to the economy of your community or tied in somehow to what you do.

Go for It!

Go to the club or organization you have targeted, state your case, and see what happens. More often than not they will be glad to work you into the schedule.

So, ask yourself: What have I got to lose? Absolutely nothing! If it does not work out, at least you have made an effort—and gotten your name out in front of that many potential prospects. Give public speaking a try. Believe me, more than one salesperson has benefited tremendously from taking this route.

Strategy #42

Pass Along Opportunities When Appropriate

What goes around comes around. This is a hard adage for a lot of salespeople to relate to but it is nevertheless a vitally important point.

Lending a Hand

Maintaining a can-do attitude where your own efforts are concerned is easy enough. But why on earth should you make an effort to help someone else out when there seems to be no logical way for that person to help you out somewhere down the line in your career?

The answer is obvious to seasoned salespeople but a little more difficult for newcomers to remember. Perhaps the best illustration I can give is to offer an example, either as a reminder or as an introduction to this important principle, that comes from the world of baseball.

Have you ever noticed that after a baseball player gets a single, he will often joke around a little bit with the first baseman on the opposing team? That is a little odd, isn't it? Considering that these are top-echelon professional competitors dealing with members of the opposition, you would expect a more stern, more compromising mindset. But there they are joking, nodding, smiling at one another.

You usually cannot hear what they are saying. Interestingly enough, it turns out that, both on the base paths and in their other contacts, opposing players often discuss some aspects of the game they play for a living. Of course, they are not giving away important strategy points that would give any competitive advantage in the game at hand. But they are often discussing points of interest that concern their own development as ballplayers. Even though they may be on opposite teams, two shortstops, for instance, will often discuss the irregularities of the surface in a given park, or pass along information on how to play a member of a third team in another city who is managing to bat a few too many hits through the infield lately.

They pass along these facts not because they do not see each other as competitors (they do!), but because they also see each other as colleagues—and it is not a bad idea to be known as the type of person who likes to help out a colleague. You might get your own hot tip on how to play that new guy who's tearing up the league! You do not know if you are going to get such a tip, but because you are "part of the grapevine" you will certainly get whatever is circulating.

Let me note here, before I am inundated with mail from baseball people about this point, that I am talking about general trends among most ballplayers. You do find the occasional hard-nosed type who refuses to share a kind word with an opposing player, but that is the exception, not the rule. Many of those tight-lipped players are rookies whose main focus is on learning the ropes and remaining in the major leagues, and not on contributing to "the book"—which is what baseball players call the collection of accepted widely circulated strategies currently influencing decisions among all teams.

Adding to "The Book"

Is there a "book" in your league? If so, do you contribute to it? Do you share insights, leads, and contacts with others where appropriate, even though you cannot see any immediate benefit in doing so? There are hundreds, probably thousands of stories of strange, off the wall, referrals generated through the grapevine that resulted in sales. To get your share, you will need to develop your reputation as a person who contributes to that common pool of resources, tips, and openings. Pass along opportunity when you can. It is a wise investment—one I never heard any salesperson regret making.

Strategy #43

Take Responsibility for Presentations That Go Haywire

Assuming personal responsibility for the sale is a remarkably effective sales tool. It works so well that, if you are like me, the first time you hear about the technique, you will probably wonder why on earth you did not incorporate it into your sales routine long ago.

To start with, you will have to be utterly, completely convinced in your own heart that you can offer your prospect the best possible solution to his problem. If that confidence is not there, the techniques I am about to describe simply will not work. If the prospect (or anyone else) asks you to talk about your firm, you have to be able to reply with sincerity that you work for a one-of-kind, customer-first company and are proud to do so.

If you think you're ready to close the sale, but you find when you try to do so that you get a roadblock and a low-information or no-information response to questions about what the problem is, you would then be well advised to simply take responsibility for whatever appears to have gone wrong in the sales process.

You read right. When you ask for the business, after having developed all the information necessary to do so, and you then hit a brick wall, you should in fact be genuinely taken aback—you should in fact be a little surprised. It should be no act. You should believe in your company so completely, and know so much about the prospect by this stage of the game, that you will be legitimately concerned at any evidence of a negative response and you will state that concern and surprise in no uncertain terms. Here is what it might sound like:

"Mr. Jones, I'm really not sure what to say. I'm quite confident that we have the best service, the best pricing, the best customization, and the best reputation of any firm in our industry. In fact, I can only think of one reason you might not decide to sign on with us today, and that is that I must have done something terribly wrong just now in giving my presentation. So, I'm going to ask you to give me a hand, Mr. Jones, and tell me where I went off course. Because, to be quite frank with you, I know this service is right for you, and I really hate to have made a mistake like that."

What do you think you will hear in response? One thing is for sure. It is not going to be easy for the prospect to come back with the run-of-the-mill brush off like, "It's just not what we were looking for." No, if you are that prospect, you will probably respect the person who had the courage to take responsibility in this way, and you will at that point pass along information on exactly what the problem is and what needs to happen next, if anything.

The common response you will hear after you take responsibility for the "no" answer in your sales cycle will sound something like this:

"No-no-no, Maureen, it has nothing to do with you. The thing is . . ."

After you hear those magic words, "The thing is . . ." you can be sure that the prospect will go into detail and start to explain the remaining obstacles to you. Then you have the facts you need to continue through the cycle.

Be Sure You Can Deliver!

Let me repeat: The above technique can be startlingly effective for uncovering what is really happening in the account, but it requires absolute faith on your part that you can in fact deliver on your promises. You also have to be willing to put aside the common fixation with "being right" that just about every human being shares, at least to a degree.

Let me ask you, though—when it comes right down to it, would you rather be "right"—or get "righted" so you get the information you need to close the sale?

Strategy #44

Control the Flow

People respond in kind; we control the flow of the conversation.

If I walk into a training room and say to the group, "Do you know what I love about your company?"—and then initiate the conversation from that point, I'm going to get a different conversation than if I walk in and say, "Let me tell you what I think needs changing around here."

The first opening is likely to open my audience up and make them feel positively inclined toward the strategies I want to share with them.

The second opening is likely to make them feel defensive and make them feel negatively inclined toward what I have to say.

People respond in kind to what they hear. When we initiate a conversation—that is to say, when we assume responsibility for the direction of the conversation, as a good salesperson must be willing to do—then we control the flow of the conversation.

This is a reliable communication principle at all points of our relationship with someone, but it is particularly important at the outset of any given conversation. How are you going to open the conversation? What question will you ask? What answer do you anticipate you will receive? What will you say then?

All too often, salespeople forget that people respond in kind, and they set up a "flow" that really doesn't support the conversation or the emerging relationship. Have you ever heard a telephone salesperson try a nifty opening such as "If I could save you eight zillion dollars, would you be interested?" How do you feel when someone asks a question like that? Don't you want to follow the (wide-open) pathway that the person has left you and answer, "No, I really have no interest in saving eight zillion dollars?"

Or what about the other common approach, the one where the salesperson asks a bland, open-ended "rapport-building" question like "How are you?" Is that really the subject you want to build the conversation around? "Well, I've got a bit of a backache actually— would you happen to know where I can get some painkillers?"

People really do respond to the subjects we raise during our conversations, so we have to choose those subjects carefully. We have to ask questions like this: "Just out of curiosity—what are you doing right now to . . . ?"

We have to take responsibility for the discussions by picking questions that focus on what the other person does—questions that lead in a direction that makes sense to both sides and improves the chance of a productive sales conversation. We really can create the flow of that conversation from the very first second of the discussion!

Strategy #45

Build Leadership Skills

Selling effectively ultimately means building leadership skills. That is not to say you should practice railroading your customers! All the confidence and authority in the world will not change a scam into an effective strategy for building trust. Building leadership skills means understanding your product or service, understanding what your prospects do for a living, and assuming responsibility for delivering results to your customers, no matter what. Prospects can sense when this is what you are offering, and they like it.

What makes a good leader?

- A good leader has a vision.
- A good leader commands respect.
- A good leader sees the big picture.
- A good leader knows when to change directions.
- A good leader points out problem areas and is ready to discuss solutions.
- A good leader has confidence in both approach and attitude.
- A good leader is accountable.
- And a good leader asks the right questions.

All of these traits are part of leadership, and I believe that leadership is an essential component of sales effectiveness.

Sometimes people challenge me on this point; they ask me what leadership really has to do with selling. After all, I'm one of those sales trainers who advocates a "consultative" approach, a selling style based on gathering very large amounts of information before you make a recommendation to a prospect. Isn't that more of a subservient model than a leadership model?

Not at all. In my view, true sales leadership requires us to ask the right questions—about what they do, where they do it, when they do it, who they do it with, why they do it that way—and then and only then asking about how we might be able to help them do it better. Once we determine, through verified information, that we can in fact help clients to do what they do better, sales leadership means saying, "Follow me!" with confidence. This is something of a balancing act, of course, but it's one that truly effective salespeople learn to perform without difficulty on a daily basis.

Strategy #46

Prepare for the Objections You'll Hear

If you were to closely evaluate your last twenty or thirty sales meetings that didn't move forward, do you think you would see any common elements to the negative responses you heard? How about the last thirty cold calls you made? Would you be able to identify any common objections in the things you heard over the phone?

Of course you would.

One of my favorite selling mottos is this one: *All responses can be anticipated!*

We spend a great deal of time focusing on this important concept in our face-to-face training programs. What it boils down to is this: You have more practice dealing with the most common negative responses you're going to hear than the prospect has in delivering them.

If you handle these common responses *differently* every time you encounter them, there's a problem somewhere!

If you've been selling for more than a month, you can probably anticipate the actual words that will be used in the negative responses you will hear from your prospect during, say, a prospecting phone call.

Will the prospect say that he's too busy to talk to you right now? That you're too expensive? That he's already happy with what he's got? That he wants you to send along some information? That he has no budget? That you probably don't have the right team in place?

You know you're going to hear these responses eventually. Why not develop a consistent approach for handling each of them?

One of our company's most common negative responses when we try to set appointments with people sounds like this: "We don't use outside trainers."

When I hear that, believe me, I don't grasp my heart and fall over in my chair from shock. It's not exactly an unexpected event. As a matter of fact, I've heard that initial negative response *so many* times that I know exactly how I'm going to try to turn it around. It sounds like this:

"Can I tell you something? That's exactly what Acme Bank said to us the first time we connected with them . . . but then they saw how we could complement what they were already doing with their internal training program, and they eventually became one of our best customers. I'd love to show you the program we put together for Acme. Why don't we meet this coming Tuesday at 2:00?"

Prepare relevant success stories: stories about satisfied customers who had exactly the same reaction but ended up working with you, stories about customers who got more value than they expected, stories about customers who benefited from a new outlook and ended up singing your team's praises. Practice these stories—they will help you turn the most common objections around.

Strategy #47

Discover What People Are Communicating Through Their Stories

All of us communicate in stories. When somebody tells you a story, that person is actually telling you the reason he or she is doing something. I have a very good friend who spent the better part of his distinguished academic career examining the question of what motivates people to share stories with one another. He realized a long time ago that all cultures tell stories, and that the aims of those stories are as valid and as important as the content of the stories themselves. Successful salespeople know how to determine the underlying motives and objectives that drive the stories prospects share with them.

Understand that the purpose of a story is to communicate something. The story you hear during a sales call has a purpose. It's virtually never there solely to entertain you.

When one prospect tells you a story about a late delivery problem he had with a previous vendor, he's telling you that schedule is important to him. When another prospect tells you a story about how tough her boss was on a colleague who couldn't make the budget numbers happen, she's telling you that she needs your help to find creative ways to address the pricing issue. When another prospect tells you about a quality control nightmare she had with her most recent vendor, she's letting you know that she needs you to work with your people to meet all of her company's specifications.

You'd be surprised how many salespeople lose sight of the purpose of the stories that prospects happen to share with them during phone calls and face-to-face meetings. My view is that there are no accidental stories during meetings with prospects. If your contact is taking the time to tell you something about how the company operates, or what his or her objective is within that company, that something is worth analyzing closely. So when you hear a story from the prospect—whether it's about a recent event in his or her professional life or an early influence on his or her career—pull out your pen and start taking notes. Jot down all the details and then ask yourself: "What's this person trying to tell me, and how can I use what I've learned to help this person do his or her job better?"

Strategy #48

Look Honestly at Your Job and Yourself

In my speeches and seminars, I often equate business with war, noting that each field of endeavor demands sound planning, has winners and losers, requires ammunition, features a chain of command, and so on. And I always conclude my remarks in this area by pointing out that business does have a few major advantages over war: Usually, nobody gets killed, and you can always change armies.

Changing armies—and the honest self-assessment that is often required to do so—are the issues at hand. If you are currently in a work environment that does not meet your personal standards for quality, ethics, or orientation toward the customer, you should consider moving on. Too often, salespeople will stay with an "army" that is all wrong for them. The reasons given can be endless—do not have time, do not have the contacts, it is not really that bad here, lack of visibility in the industry—but, in the final analysis, they are all rationalizations and unconvincing ones at that.

There is a danger here, because sometimes salespeople, who are a persuasive lot, will often go to great lengths to sell themselves on an idea. If that idea does not really work, the possibility of denial and self-deception looms. You may have to be on your guard, and make a special effort to be brutally honest with yourself about the direction both you and your firm are headed in. Why? Because it is your career on the line. You want to work toward developing productive, mutually beneficial relationships with all the people you encounter on a professional level. If you find that your sales network is not doing that for you—if you find that to the contrary you are leaving a trail of angry former customers in your wake—you are asking for trouble.

Some salespeople try to play games with themselves. They try to rationalize a situation that is inherently manipulative or abusive. They delude themselves about the nature of the reality they are building into their lives. Do not be one of them. Do not set yourself up for a fall.

You have to feel a sense of mission in your gut. You have to believe in your cause. You have to know in the marrow of your bones that all of your efforts are in line with your value system. You have to know that that system encourages only productive, straight shooter interactions. However you identify your goals, you must be certain that it is morally right for you to pursue them. You must know instinctively the benefit people will derive from working with you, and you must believe in your heart that all your company's efforts are for the best.

Otherwise you may well find that you have some difficulty succeeding.

Strategy #49

Tell Everyone You Meet Who You Work for and What You Sell

Why not? Why not tell your doctor? Your electrician? Your dentist? The cab driver you rode with this morning? Your friend at another company? The person you sit next to on the airplane? Your barber? Members of the community group or charitable organization you work with? The guy who has the seat next to you at the ballgame?

Why not make a point of broadcasting your profession to anyone and everyone—with pride? I'm not suggesting you subject everyone you know to a sales pitch, of course. What I am suggesting is that it become second nature for you to say, loud and clear, to every single person you meet, bar none, that you're a salesperson for XYZ Corporation, maker of the finest widgets west of the Pecos. Couple that with a handshake and a confident look-you-in-the-eye smile, and you know what? Every once in a while, someone's going to say, "Widgets, huh? You know, we've been thinking about those . . ."

In my opinion, far too many salespeople have a pathological aversion to letting people know what they do for a living. The only reason I can come up with for this is that we often aren't quite as proud of what we do for a living as a brain surgeon might be, or an attorney, or an editor, or a scientist, or a teacher, or workers in any of the dozens of categories who have no difficulty mentioning how they spend the majority of their waking hours.

We should be proud of being salespeople; I know I am! I know that the economy of the society I live in would not function without people who do what I do for a living, and I know that every transaction I undertake benefits all who are affected by it. Am I proud of that? You bet!

Strategy #50

Keep Your Sense of Humor

Let's be honest. It can be tough to be a salesperson. Paradoxically enough, that's exactly why sales work has to be funny now and then.

I can only pass along my own observations about the salespeople I've worked with: Laughing helps. And not just around the edges. Laughing helps a lot. Salespeople depend on a good self-image more than any other professionals I know of, and it's awfully hard to keep a good self-image if you take yourself so seriously that you can't back off and laugh about the world once in awhile.

Let me backtrack for a moment. One of the most scathing arguments against becoming a salesperson I know of is a very depressing film I saw some years back called *Salesman*. It's a documentary shot in grainy black and white about three traveling salespeople. It portrays sales as manipulative, dishonest work—work that no thinking, feeling person would ever undertake voluntarily.

I have a real problem with that movie, for a couple of reasons. The first is that a great many people who aren't salespeople have been exposed to it, and have formed unrealistic stereotypes about my profession as a result. The second is that most of us who are salespeople haven't been exposed to it, and haven't been able to see the debilitating results of consistently bad sales work. This movie is convincing proof of how dangerous a salesperson with the wrong attitude can be, both to customers and to the salesperson who takes work very, very seriously—that movie will probably have a remarkable effect on you once you see it.

The salespeople in this film make just about every mistake in the book, including, but not limited to, failing to establish customer goals, lying to prospects, not listening to prospects, carrying a negative mental attitude, and failing to commit to their own ongoing professional development. But there is another area that, if it were rectified, could make all the other problems manageable.

They take the damned job too seriously and never give themselves a chance to decompress. It is difficult to attend to those other (potentially catastrophic) problems if they have become a part of your sales environment, but I can guarantee you that it is absolutely impossible to approach your sales work the way it should be approached if you cannot step back and laugh at yourself once in a while, preferably while on the job.

You are too important a tool to yourself to run down. Take a break. Remember that you have to take the long view, and that today's catastrophe usually does not mean much tomorrow. This is a message that really never got to sink in as far as the salespeople in this movie were concerned, and they paid for it.

Don't let the World At Large talk you into thinking that you are not in charge of your day, your month, or your career. After all, you are the one with the answers; you are the professional solver of problems; you are the one who stays in control by keeping your head, asking the right questions, and being precise when it comes to giving necessary advice. Lighten up and win! And remember: Success could not happen to a nicer person.

Strategy #51

Beware of Bad Advice on the Internet

The Internet has changed the way many people sell. Few of us could have imagined, six or seven years ago, how easy it would become to gain access to some of the most vital daily selling information. Researching a company? You can now check for its Web site easily. Hungry for new leads? Dozens of online resources can point you toward new people and companies to contact. Looking for advice on how to improve your selling technique? Hundreds of (self-appointed) sales experts are only a click away.

And this is where you can get yourself into trouble. Too many sales "gurus" use their sites to dispense advice that can sabotage the job of building a relationship with your prospect. Consider the following:

Here's an example of bad advice: *Don't work with the prospect to develop a plan that "makes sense"—instead, use pressure tactics.* A site we visited encouraged salespeople to ask this question when face-to-face with a hesitant contact: "Now, don't you agree that this product can help you or would be of benefit to you?" Ouch. A better approach would be to ask, "What exactly are you trying to get accomplished in this area?"

More bad advice: *Find the pain.* Several sites we encountered advised salespeople to use questions to plant subliminal "hints" designed to get prospects to reveal that they actually hate their current vendor. Examples: "Do you also worry about . . .?" "How tough a position does that put you in?" Instead of trying to find the pain—which may or may not exist—salespeople should focus on finding out what the prospect actually does.

And still more bad advice: *Always be closing.* This outdated maxim showed up as constructive advice on more than one of the sales sites we visited, as did any number of manipulative closing "tricks" that will quickly destroy emerging relationships. More pragmatic advice: "Always be asking questions."

It's too easy for people to set up a Web site—which makes it hard to find a good one with relevant, responsible information for salespeople. Beware of the advice you take from the Internet.

Strategy #52

Use Company Events to Move the Relationship Forward

"Thanks for calling to confirm—but I'm afraid I'm going to have to cancel our meeting for next week. We've decided to put a hold on all our spending in this area for now. We'll be re-evaluating in a couple of months. Keep in touch, all right?"

It's part of the sales landscape—a law as dependable as gravity. No matter how effective, persuasive, or experienced a given salesperson is, some percentage of that person's promising leads will turn into "opportunities." These are static contacts that aren't moving through the sales process and can't be counted on to provide income—at least for the time being.

The question really isn't whether contacts will fall into the opportunity category but what steps to take when they do. How do you reignite interest and generate activity within your list of "cold" prospects? Marty, one of our sales representatives, came up with an interesting strategy.

Marty decided to write a letter to every prospect who had decided not to buy from him over a given period. Basically, the letter said this: "It was a pleasure meeting with you a while back to talk about what your company was doing. Even though we were unable to move forward at that time, I'm still thinking about you."

Marty then invited each cold contact to sit in at one of his company's upcoming events. "This will give you an opportunity to evaluate, first-hand, how applicable what we do is to your business environment," he wrote. "Attached is a list of all upcoming training where my clients have approved outside observers. I've also included a brief description of each of the programs."

According to Marty, he got calls from prospects that were very interested in observing specific programs, even though they had initially declined his firm's services.

The letter-writing strategy had another application as well. Marty decided to write to each member of his active client base and extend the same invitation. The letter began as follows: "First of all, let me thank you for allowing us to work with you and XYZ Company. We are very excited to have you as part of our client list, as you are a significant player. It is for this reason that I would like to extend the following invitation to you . . . ."

As his flurry of return calls proved, Marty's innovative letter technique is an effective way to win back (or solidify) your position on the to-do lists of your customers and inactive leads. His idea can be adapted to training programs, open houses, media events, and any number of other occasions.

Strategy #53

Follow the "Yes"

"I'm spending too much time with leads that don't seem to turn into anything. How can I tell who's really interested in working with my organization?"

First and foremost, let's define what we mean by "prospect." A prospect is someone who is willing to take an active step—demonstrated by a specific time commitment—to talk seriously about the possibility of working with you.

That's an extremely important definition. Do yourself—and your career—a favor: Commit it to memory!

The most effective salespeople learn to spot people who aren't giving them a clear "yes" answer to follow, and distinguish those people from the rest of the world. The trick is to understand that the relevant yes answers take many important forms before the close, but virtually always include some kind of time commitment:

- "Yes, I'll meet with you next Tuesday at three o'clock."
- "Yes, I'll introduce you to my boss next Monday morning."
- "Yes, I'll take a look at your notes and tell you what works and what doesn't. Let's schedule a conference call."

- "Yes, I'll schedule a meeting with the full committee. When are you free?"
- "Yes, we'd like you to start on January first."

No book can teach you how to make a prospect do something he or she doesn't want to do. If you follow the advice that appears below, however, you will make the most of your time and maximize the number of prospects who decide to tell you what to do—by giving you business.

Here are the three steps you can take right now to begin following the yes.

Step One

Make a habit of "throwing out the ball" (suggesting a Next Step) to a number of people each and every day. Throwing out the ball might sound like this: "I'd love to get together with you to talk about what we've done with the XYZ Company. Can we meet Tuesday at three o'clock at your office?"

(By the way, if you're interested in taking advantage of online courses in Appointment Making, Prospect Management, or High Efficiency Selling, you can find out more about those training resources at *www.dei-sales.com*. Our Web site offers full-scale online overviews of all of our in-person training programs.)

Step Two

Learn to distinguish "sounds like YES" answers from "actual YES" answers.

"Actual YES" answers are ones in which the person agrees to a clear next step with you, complete with date and time, that's scheduled for the near future (typically, within the next two weeks). Actual YES answers could sound like this:

You:	*Can we get together Wednesday at two o'clock to talk about this further?*
Prospect:	*Wednesday's no good for me; what about Friday morning?*

Or they could sound like this:

You:	*Why don't you and I meet with your supplier next week to set up a plan?*
Prospect:	*You know what? That's a great idea. When are you free?*

Step Three

Treat everything that's not an actual YES as though it were an actual NO.

Here's the really critical point: Stop wasting time with people who are not actually moving through the sales process with you. So even if the person says, "Call me sometime next month," we put that person lower on the priority list than someone who says, "Let's talk next Monday at two o'clock."

The bottom line: Invest your time wisely, move on to someone new, and stop spinning your wheels.

Strategy #54

Know When to Say, "I Didn't Anticipate That"

Some days you might feel this way: "I just had the worst meeting of my life. I had no idea what to say when the prospect shot me down. What can I do in a situation like that?"

The most successful salespeople work from the principle that all responses are anticipated. What does that mean? It means that, as professionals, we've had enough conversations with enough people over the years to develop a reliable sense of what's likely to happen next during an exchange with a prospect or customer. Put more bluntly, experienced salespeople don't get taken by surprise all that often. If that's a fact of sales life—and it is—we can actually use this principle to our advantage in turning around the negative responses we hear.

Consider the following scenario. Alan, a young sales representative in the telecommunications industry, meets with Bill, a middle-aged MIS director at a *Fortune* 100 company. At the end of the first meeting, Alan says to the prospect, "I think this meeting went well. Why don't we set a meeting for next Tuesday at three o'clock so I can show you a plan of how we might be able to work together?" And then the roof seems to fall in.

"Alan," Bill says, "why don't we do it this way. If you want to, you can go ahead and e-mail your information to me, and I'll call you back if I'm interested."

What should Alan do? Suppose Alan were to try to explain why he wanted to meet again? How would that go over? More than likely, Bill—the senior person in the conversation—would get annoyed. He might even suggest that Alan do a little more homework about his industry before attempting to continue the conversation. But consider another approach, one that emphasizes Alan's experience in the world of sales, levels the playing field, and points the relationship in a positive direction.

Suppose that, when Bill puts up a roadblock by saying something like, "Go ahead and e-mail the information to me instead," Alan looks a little startled. There's a brief pause. Then Alan says, "Gee, I really didn't anticipate that you would say that."

What happens next? Ninety-five times out of a hundred, if Alan says that and stops talking, Bill will ask a neutral question—like, "Really, why not?" Suddenly, the playing field is level!

Alan can now say, "Well, frankly, our conversation was going so well, I really expected a different outcome. Usually, at this stage of the conversation, people say they want to meet with me again. Just out of curiosity . . . why wouldn't you want to meet with me again?"

By saying, "I didn't anticipate that," and then asking for guidance in this way, you'll usually get much better information about exactly where you stand with the prospect. And that's what you want: the right information.

For instance, in this scenario, Bill might say, "Well, the truth is, Alan, we have to deal with an urgent project right now, and I can't even think about making any major telecom decision this quarter." Alan might reply, "Okay—when do you think you will be ready to continue our discussion?" Bill might set an appointment for the following month, instead of the following week—and the relationship would be moving forward. All because he said, "I really didn't anticipate that you would say that!"

Using this skill is part of a larger process I call "getting righted." It's one of the most important (and most frequently overlooked) steps in selling. If I say, "I didn't anticipate that you would say that," what I'm really saying is, "Help me out—I must have missed something. Tell me where I went wrong." In fact, I can use exactly those kinds of words to ask overtly for guidance from the prospect. I can also take advantage of the prospect's natural instinct to correct me by stating something I suspect isn't true and watching carefully for the reaction I get. ("Now, it sounds to me like your timing priorities might be to get this project in place by this spring." "Oh, no, we're trying to get moving much more quickly than that—by December 15th at the very latest.")

Recently, I was training a large group of sales representatives who worked in the communications industry. During the question-and-answer session, one of them said to me, "We never seem to get the information we need from the people we visit. They find direct questions intrusive. What's the best way to get someone to open up to you?"

I told him, "Make a mistake."

He stared at me for a moment, as though I were mad to suggest such a thing. Then I explained what I meant.

"If you build a mistake into your question," I said, "the other person's instinct will automatically be to correct you. By allowing yourself to be righted, you will get the right information, and the other person will be in a position of strength. The conversation will flow naturally, because you've allowed the other person to be correct."

As it happens, this is a strategy we teach all of our own salespeople. If we're interested in learning the name of a prospect's most important competitor, we won't just ask, "Who's your most important competitor?" Instead, we'll say something like this: "I'm just curious—who do you consider to be your most significant competition. Would it be Flapjack Industries?" (This is assuming that we have a good idea that Flapjack Industries is not the company's most important competitor.)

The prospect instantly offers a correction: "Oh, no, it's not Flapjack—they're much too small for us to worry about. We're up against a much bigger outfit. Our main competition is ABC Industries."

Can you see how it works? Within just a few seconds, we've built rapport, allowed the other person a position of dominance in the conversation, and uncovered an essential piece of information.

Not long ago, this "build in a mistake" strategy helped one of our reps secure a major series of training dates from a huge electronics firm that was preparing its people for a new product launch. By carefully incorporating a few faulty assumptions within the questioning sequence, we were able to get information that had not been released to our competitors—information we used to develop a customized proposal that landed an account worth several hundred thousand dollars. To win that sale, we had to put aside the salesperson's typical concern for "being right" and find a way to get corrected!

With a few thoughtfully constructed questions and a little practice, you can take advantage of this powerful questioning strategy. Try it!

Don't worry about being "right"—get righted. The idea of including a conscious mistake while interviewing a client may seem unorthodox, but doing so can point you toward information you won't get in any other way.

"Getting righted" (by saying something like "I didn't anticipate you'd say that," or "Help me figure out where I went wrong," or "It seems to me that such-and-such is a priority for you") can be an extremely effective information-gathering strategy. Use it to get the prospect to react, and you will be more likely to determine what is really going on in the relationship—and how it should move forward.

Strategy #55

Beware of "Casual Friday"

Recently I received this question: "I'm visiting a prospect next Friday who has informed me that once a week, team members at his organization 'dress down' for casual day. This Friday is such a day. In order to fit in, should I yield to my instinct to wear jeans and a turtleneck when I go in for my appointment?"

The answer: No!

This is an issue on which we've had a good deal of first-hand experience at my company. The evidence is overwhelming: You cannot win—and can only lose—if you opt to "go casual" during a visit to a prospect's facility. No matter what the prospect says, no matter what the weather outside your window looks like, no matter how comfortable you feel with your contact, your best option is always to dress professionally for sales appointments.

The same principle, of course, applies to companies you visit where "casual day" extends into "casual week"—in other words, workplaces where everyone, from the head of the company on down, makes a habit of showing up for work each and every day in chinos, T-shirts, or similarly "relaxed" attire. Even when visiting such a workplace, dressing to "match" the laid-back fashion standards of your prospects is a big mistake.

Why? Consider these points:

- First and foremost, by dressing casually, you send the wrong message about your role. As a salesperson, you are going up against the status quo—that which the company is already doing. Never forget: You are a messenger of professional change. That means your recommendations must not be mistaken for those of an employee, and they should certainly not be mistaken for those of a mere social acquaintance. Think consultant—not beach buddy. After all, which one would you trust with the future of your business?

- Second, by dressing casually, you send the message that nothing special is happening. Something special is happening. You've shown up!

- Third, by dressing casually, you reduce your negotiating leverage. When you're finalizing a fee structure or winning a critical date on the calendar, aren't you more comfortable bringing all the authority and impact you can possibly muster to the discussion?

- Fourth, by dressing casually, you send the wrong message to your own employer—and to anyone of importance who may stroll through your facilities while you're dressed to underwhelm. ("Why on earth is he dressed like that today?") Perhaps the laid-back company wants to hire you because of the great job you did. Great! That still doesn't mean you should dress like Oscar Madison on the sales call. The only time you should ever dress casually is when you spend the entire day in your own office—and everyone else is doing the same.

- Finally, notice that, by dressing casually, you reduce your options for the rest of the day. Even if you haven't put off the prospect at Company A by dressing like a shlub (and how certain can you ever be about that?), what about the prospect at Company B? When you limit your opportunities, you limit your earning power!

Sure, regional standards for appropriate business attire will vary. Sure, you'll dress differently when networking at a cocktail party than when networking at a trade show. Regardless, dressing down costs you money.

Taking the time and care to dress well for a meeting is universally understood business shorthand for "You should take what I'm saying seriously." Send that message!

Some salespeople say that dressing down makes them feel more "comfortable" because it constitutes "following the prospect's lead." (A side note: These are often the same salespeople who don't follow the prospect's lead when they're invited to coffee or lunch by a prospect; they're afraid they'll do something wrong, and they miss out on a chance to deepen the relationship.)

Let me close this chapter with a personal observation. All dressing down does for me is to remind me that I'm not earning what I could be. I don't know about you, but I'm not really comfortable with that! That's why we have a strict "dress-for-business" role at my company for sales reps preparing to go out on appointments—and we always will.

Never "go casual" during a meeting with a prospect.

Strategy #56

Ask Key Questions about
Your Best Accounts

Recently, a client of ours in the telecommunications industry asked us to help set up a customized training program to help sales representatives increase sales depth within its base of existing customers. This client had numerous *Fortune* 100 customers—but had not developed a systemized way of identifying new areas for growth within each of these major accounts.

At the session, we asked participants to answer the following questions about each account:

- How can I work with this company's sales department to win new customers—and increase profitability? *Follow-up:* What new people within the organization would I talk to about new customer development?
- How can I help the target company's sales, customer service, shipping, and transportation departments to maintain its base of existing accounts more effectively? *Follow-up:* What new people within the organization would I talk to about maintaining existing accounts?
- How can I work with the target company's shipping, accounts receivable, accounts payable, and manufacturing departments to improve communi-

cations with major suppliers? *Follow-up:* What new people within the organization would I talk to about improving communications with suppliers?

- What programs can I put together with this company's marketing and sales departments to help the organization gain a competitive edge in the marketplace? *Follow-up:* What new people within the organization would I talk to about improving the company's competitive position?

- How can I help this company's department heads and human resources people retain and recruit high-quality employees? *Follow-up:* What new people within the organization would I talk to about human resource issues?

- What can I propose to this company's shipping, receiving, dispatching, sales, and customer service people to help streamline transportation? *Follow-up:* What new people within the organization would I talk to about streamlining transportation activities?

In answering these questions, trainees were asked to identify contacts in at least five different areas within each company. They wrote down the size of each account, the possible product application by division/department, and information in each relevant area gleaned from sources like the Internet or the company's annual report.

At the end of this process, all the participants had a huge number of new prospects! Their new calling list was prioritized according to three criteria: territory management considerations (i.e., which contacts to meet with in the same building on a given day), the potential account size, and the likely time cycle. We then showed these reps how to build their calls around the groups and people they had helped in the past, thus dramatically increasing their likelihood of scheduling a meeting with the new person.

The bottom line: By asking these questions, you will be able to target and win new business within your major accounts—and beat quota.

Strategy #57

Find Out What's Changed

Some months ago, I wandered into a Brooks Brothers store. My aim was simple: I wanted to buy a pair of suspenders. That was all I wanted to buy. The gentleman at the counter stared at me blankly when I stepped up and looked at him. Apparently, I thought to myself, I'm supposed to speak first. So I said, "I'm here to buy some suspenders." He pointed and said, "Over there."

Having received my marching orders, I walked in the direction he had pointed. I picked out a single pair of suspenders. I paid for them. I left the store. That was the end of the exchange.

A week or so later, I went to an electronics store. Once again, my aim was simple: I wanted to buy a basic clock radio. (You know the kind: They run about $20.) A clock radio was all I wanted to buy. I meandered into the store. I stepped over to the counter and looked at the woman by the cash register. Although I was ready to speak first (my experience with the Brooks Brothers attendant had taught me something), I found to my surprise that, this time, I wasn't going to have to.

"Hi, there," the woman behind the counter said, smiling.

"Hi," I replied. "Can you show me where to find a $20 clock radio?"

Please bear in mind that that really was all I wanted to buy. And yet, at that point in the conversation, something amazing happened. The woman behind the counter said, "Sure. Just out of curiosity, though . . . what brings you to the store today?"

What a great question! She was actually interested in what had recently changed in my life. Clearly, something had changed enough to make me decide to walk into her store. She wasn't clear on precisely what it was, and she wanted to find out. So she asked. (After all, the odds were against my walking into the store on a Monday morning because I had nothing better to do, right?)

I answered her (refreshingly conversational) question by explaining that I had just moved to an apartment nearby, and that, since the apartment was bare, I had no way of waking up on time in the morning.

She smiled and showed me where the clock radios were. I picked out a model. Then she asked me whether I wanted to look at a television set. Well, that certainly made sense. I was camping out in an empty apartment; I was likely to be in California for a while, which meant I was in the market for a television; I'd already made the trip down to the electronics store. Why not at least take a look at a floor model or two? "Sure," I said. "Why don't you show me where those are and let me take a look at what you have." There were other questions as well. Did I want to look at CD players? Microwave ovens?

Cordless telephones?

An hour after having walked into a store intending only to buy a $20 clock radio, I left with $2,000 in merchandise. All because one person had the sense to ask me about what I had done that had caused me to change my pattern and walk into her store.

Do you know what has recently changed in your prospect's or customer's life? When somebody calls you "out of the blue," do you ask some variation on "Just out of curiosity—what made you decide to call us today?"

Ask prospects "do-based" questions that focus on what has changed in their world. Do-based questions focus on what the other person is trying to accomplish, is doing right now, or has done in the past. For instance, "I'm just curious. What made you decide to get in touch with us?" That's a great strategy for salespeople—and anyone who interacts with customers and prospects.

Strategy #58

Use E-mail Intelligently

Here are ten proven strategies for using e-mail persuasively with prospects and customers:

1. Use a spell-check program. Read every e-mail message at least two times before you send it. For particularly important messages, compose your message in a word processor and print out a copy. Ask a colleague to check your style and spelling before you send the message.

2. Review both the topic and the content of your message closely before you send it. Ask yourself whether your e-mail message is appropriate for all the individuals to whom it could be forwarded in a given organization. Remember that it is easy for your recipient to send your message to dozens or hundreds of people. If you're passing along performance assessments, remarks about company politics, or "frank" opinions about the people in your world or your prospect's world, think twice before you transmit those sensitive messages via e-mail.

3. Never use all lowercase or all capital letters in an e-mail message. Find other ways to impart a relaxed tone or to add emphasis to your writing. Adopting an informal tone is fine; on the other hand, varying from the rules of standard written English, while sometimes appropriate, will generally detract from the overall level of professionalism of your message.

4. Archive messages you need for your records; delete the rest. Good file maintenance eliminates confusion and reduces the chances of mistakenly forwarding a message to the wrong person.

5. Include a clear, concise, and inviting headline in the subject line. The best kind of headline builds interest by helping the reader identify both the topic of your message and its relevance. (For example: "Directions to next week's sales training program.")

6. Include your name and contact information when sending or responding to e-mail. Your e-mail management software includes a feature that allows you to compose a consistent electronic "signature" that appears automatically at the end of each message. Use this feature as "virtual stationery" that identifies you, establishes your position within your organization, and passes along your contact information.

7. Check your own e-mail daily. In today's business environment, this is just as important as checking your phone messages!

8. When writing for distribution to a large group, protect the privacy of your recipients' addresses by entering them on the "BCC:" line, rather than the "CC:" line. "BCC" stands for "blind carbon copy." Addresses entered on this line do not appear within the message. (If you wish to specify who is receiving a message without disclosing everyone's e-mail address, you can include the full names of your intended recipients at the beginning of your message.)

9. Avoid sending hasty responses to inquiries you receive via e-mail. A curt, one-sentence response to a customer, contact, or colleague is easier to send than most people imagine; such a message may be misinterpreted. If you don't have time to respond in full to a question or problem, say so in your e-mail message and follow up appropriately later.

10. Think twice. Never send an e-mail message composed in anger.

Strategy #59

When in Doubt,
Ask for the Appointment

How can you get more face-to-face appointments with prospects?
Ask for them!

I make appointments with any and every salesperson who calls
me to ask for a face-to-face meeting. I don't screen my calls. I don't
make salespeople jump through hoops. If they want to meet with
me, I try to meet with them.

This is a rule I've developed over the years. I make a point of living up to it—as long as the travel demands of my training schedule
don't make it impossible for me to do so. The ground rules are very
simple: If I'm going to be in my New York office, and you call me up
and ask me for a meeting, I'll schedule a slot for you. It may be an
early appointment, and it may not be for that week, but you will get
a commitment for a face-to-face appointment.

I take this approach because I like to see and hear what real, live
salespeople are doing. If they've come across a strategy that works
on the phone or in person, I want to know about it. By the same
token, if they're doing something that doesn't work, I want to know
about that, too.

Here's the million-dollar question. If all any salesperson has to do to get a meeting with me is call me up, why do I end up scheduling so few meetings with salespeople?

Take last week. I had hardly any travel commitments, and I spent almost the entire week in my New York City office. And yet I didn't sit down with a single outside salesperson.

That wasn't because I hadn't received calls from salespeople over the previous weeks. I had! Sometimes I get half a dozen of those calls in a single day. The problem is that I only schedule appointments with people who come out and ask me for a meeting—and hardly anyone ever asks me directly for an appointment!

Instead, they hem and haw and ask all kinds of "probing questions" that distract them from the purpose of their call. That purpose, presumably, is to set an appointment with me so the two of us can sit down and talk about whether it would make sense for me to use their product or service. Somehow this topic hardly ever comes up.

It's become something of a running joke around our office. I always put the calls on speakerphone so people can hear how callers will do everything except ask for a meeting. Everyone on my staff knows that all the salesperson has to do is suggest a date and time—I'll say "Yes." But for some reason the salespeople I speak to have a very hard time actually suggesting an appointment.

Here's an actual recent example of such a phone call. Someone calls me up and asks, "Are you currently investing in the stock market?"

I say, "Yes."

He says, "Are you using a broker right now?"

I say, "Yes."

He says, "Are you investing in such and such an area?"

I say, "Yes."

He says, "Would you mind if I sent you some materials about our company?"

I say, "No, I wouldn't mind that."

At that point, he says "Thank you" and tells me he hopes we can meet face to face very soon. Then he hangs up!

If he'd simply asked me, "Can we set up a meeting?" my answer would have been "Yes!"

How many other relationships could these salespeople move forward by focusing a little less on those "probing questions"? How many people might they meet if they actually made a direct request for a meeting during a cold call?

Don't get distracted by so-called probing questions at the opening stage of the relationship. Ask directly for an appointment when you make prospecting calls.

Strategy #60

Raise Tough Issues Yourself

If you go into a meeting and have a "gut feeling" that a prospect has doubts about some aspect of working with you, how do you confirm your instinct? Most salespeople hesitate to ask a person directly for an opinion; they initiate a long discussion about other topics instead of directly raising important questions. This approach is usually counterproductive, and always a waste of time.

Suppose you meet with a prospect and think that his or her biggest issue about using your products is resistance to your price. Here's the four-step strategy to use:

1. Say that you are unhappy or concerned.
2. Wait for the prospect to ask "Why?" (He or she always will.)
3. Raise the issue you're unsure about briefly.
4. Listen to the prospect's response.

For instance: On your next meeting, you might decide to walk into the prospect's office, sit down, and say, "I'm really concerned," and then stop talking. The decision-maker will reply, "Why?" Your answer: "Because I don't think my price is competitive."

You've raised the issue yourself. This type of statement will allow the prospect to respond honestly. Count on it: If you listen to the decision-maker, you will soon know exactly what he or she thinks about your pricing.

A client in the health-care industry called me the other day. She was uncertain about the status of an upcoming enrollment with a major prospect. She and her prospect had tentatively discussed setting an enrollment meeting with the target company's employees for the following month, but there had been no action.

Was there a problem? Was the prospect planning to put off the enrollment indefinitely? If not, why had there been no action?

The question we faced was really a pretty simple one: Did the prospect have a timing obstacle, and, if so, what was it? On my advice, our client called her prospect and said, "I'm concerned about the enrollment for August that we discussed."

The prospect said, "Really? Why is that?"

"I'm afraid that we don't have enough time to get this meeting together for you," our client answered.

The prospect responded, "You know what? I'm concerned, too. Let's set the dates right now." Problem solved!

Take a good look at your current prospect base. Are you uncertain about a prospect's reaction to your pricing? Call that person right now and use the four-step process you've just learned to raise the pricing issue. Are you concerned about a person's level of comfort with a product's warranty? Use this strategy to raise the issue yourself; listen closely to what you hear in response. Are you unsure whether a prospect agrees with your assessment of a product's scalability? Raise the issue yourself!

Follow the four steps. I guarantee that you will get a reaction from the other person that lets you know immediately what you have to focus on.

Here's an alternative approach that uses basically the same principle. Sometimes I'll find myself walking a new prospect through a preliminary proposal, and I won't have any idea what the prospect thinks of my pricing. (Actually, this doesn't happen all that often, as I've picked up some skill over the years at reading people's body language, but it does happen from time to time.) When I have absolutely no idea what the person's reaction to my pricing is, and the relationship is a little too young for me to feel comfortable with the "I'm concerned" approach, I may say something else. I may say, "You know, this is the point where people typically have a problem with price if that's an issue for them." Then I stop talking.

What have I done? I've just given the person permission to talk about my pricing. Nine times out of ten, he or she will open up. The person's response to this simple statement virtually always tells me where I stand.

Remember, it is your job to uncover the real issue at hand! Many prospects will say that they object to pricing, while they are really covering up some other concern. It is your responsibility to ask questions and determine what (if anything) is preventing you from working together.

Use this simple strategy to find out exactly where a prospect stands on any given issue. You don't have to initiate a long discussion. All you have to do is raise the issue. As you will learn quickly, the prospect or customer will do most of the talking!

Strategy #61

Use an Effective Strategy for Getting Return Phone Calls

Many salespeople don't bother to leave a voicemail message, even in this day and age! You should always leave a message for your contact when you're making prospecting calls. My bet is that if you leave the right kind of message, you're more likely to get a curious call back. That puts the contact in a better mindset to consider meeting with you.

Here are two strategies to implement that will improve your return-call results immediately.

75 Percent Return Calls

The following message format has resulted in 75 percent return calls. Use it!

"Hi, it's Bob Black—my number is 212-555-1212, and I'm calling from ABC Company. This is regarding the Huge Customer of Ours in Your Industry. I look forward to speaking with you soon."

This assumes, of course, that the company you reference is one of your satisfied customers. When the person calls back, you must use the work you've done with the company you mentioned as your reason for the call.

99 Percent Return Calls

If you are calling someone who has been called by a rep in your company, use that person as the reference in your message.

"Hi, it's Bob Black. I'm calling you about our representative, Jane Myers, who spoke to you last month. Please call me at 212-555-1212."

This technique has resulted in 99 percent return calls! When you get the call back, you can simply say, "My records show that Jane spoke with you last month about working with us—and I wanted to find out where things went wrong." You will find that two very interesting things happen when you do this. First, the contact will become extremely protective of the person he or she met with. Second, the person you're calling will almost always reveal exactly what is standing in the way of your working together—even if he or she avoided discussing this with your colleague in the past. The person's explanation will usually begin with the words, "The thing is . . ."

When you start using the message strategies I've outlined above, you will want to make a habit of keeping easy-to-retrieve notes on who you're calling and why. If you get taken by surprise by a return call (and it's a pretty good bet that you will), you can retain momentum in the conversation by saying:

"Ms. Jones, thank you so much for returning my call—let me get my notes for you. Would you mind holding on for just a moment?"

This is an honest, direct, and completely professional request that will win you the few seconds you need to grab your file, notebook, or Palm Pilot and retrieve the information you need to reorient yourself.

Use these two simple strategies to dramatically increase the number of return calls you get when you leave messages.

Strategy #62

Don't Bring Everything!

Recently, a participant in one of my training programs asked me: "I don't know what to say at the end of the appointment. The prospect tells me we've covered everything in detail and that he/she needs to talk to other people about what my organization offers. I can't seem to get a next step. What do I do?"

There are a number of reasons meetings with promising prospects don't result in a next step. However, one of the most common problems in this area—having no reason to come back—is also one of the easiest to fix.

Think about it. When we've "covered everything" with the prospect, we appear to have left ourselves no reason to come back for that all-important second meeting! Solution: Don't cover everything during the first meeting with the prospect!

Specifically, don't bring everything. Bring enough in the way of testimonials, references, articles, books, and similar sales tools to give your meeting a purpose and a sense of structure. But leave something for the second meeting, so you can say something like this as the meeting draws to a close:

"You know what? You really ought to take a look at what we've been doing in the area of customized training for people in the widget industry. I should bring you some of the materials we've put together on that. Why don't I come by again next Tuesday at two o'clock and show you one of the projects we've been working on?"

If you bring the essentials—and only the essentials—to your initial meeting with a prospect, you'll have a built-in "reason to come back." If you make the most of it, you'll run into fewer prospects that will tell you that they've heard everything they need to hear during the first meeting.

Resist the temptation to bring everything to the first meeting; leave yourself a reason to come back for the second one.

Strategy #63

Don't "Product Dump"

Not long ago, I got this question: "I give what I think is a great opening summary of my company and its products and services during the opening phase of the first meeting. It takes fifteen to twenty minutes. Prospects don't seem to be responding well to it, though. What's happening?"

The answer was simple. "What's happening is you're forgetting one of the most important facts of professional sales: You are more than a walking brochure!"

Most salespeople are taught to "find the needs" of their prospects, so they can make presentations designed to show how their organizations can fill those needs. In fact, they get used to six or eight common needs and become very comfortable indeed discussing them.

There's a problem with this approach, though. It turns you into a walking advertisement. You recite a familiar "spiel" during your first meeting. Guess what? In today's economy, the odds are high that your prospect already has—or has access to—some variation on what you offer. He or she doesn't really need you at all.

The act of reciting a well-known (and lengthy) monologue to a prospect is called "throwing up" on the prospect—or, to use a slightly more pleasant term, executing a "product dump." Whatever we call it, it means we are sending far more information out during the first meeting than we are taking in. In fact, product dumping is the most common reason for a first meeting with a prospect not to go well. Prospects hate hearing a product dump during the first meeting. (Don't you?)

Reciting what we think we know about familiar needs during initial meetings with prospects won't help us to sell more efficiently. In assessing people's needs, we usually assume we know all about their business already. We assume that this prospect is facing exactly the same situation as the last prospect we met with. So we just soliloquize about what we have to offer or read from a brochure. In so doing, we overlook opportunities to gather meaningful information about what's actually going on in the life of the person we're talking to. The result: another turned-off prospect.

The reason so many salespeople rely on product dumps is that meetings with prospects can be stressful. When we're stressed, we fall back on what's familiar to us—namely, what we know about our product or service. Unfortunately, when we do that, we close down the lines of communication.

Not long ago, we had a visit from a salesperson who represented a copier company. The meeting consisted of a brief exchange of greetings, a couple of superficial remarks about the weather and the traffic, and the salesperson's spiel about the features of his machine. This spiel went on, uninterrupted, for twenty minutes, at the conclusion of which time the fellow tried to "close" me. He didn't succeed. He tried again. He didn't succeed. He packed up his things and left.

Why do I share this story with you? Because I want you to understand the real reason I didn't even consider buying from this young man. He never asked me what business I was in.

Can you imagine? Here he is trying to sell me a $15,000 copier, and he has no idea what I plan to use it for!

Don't try to sell that way. Don't let your nervousness shut down the possibility of learning the most elementary facts about the person you're talking to. Don't miss out on a chance to find out a little bit more about your prospect than that stressed-out copier salesperson did.

In the next two chapters, you'll find strategies for conducting a great face-to-face discussion with your prospect.

Avoid product dumps. They turn prospects off.

Strategy #64

Move Beyond "Slapshot" Selling

Has this ever happened to you? "I just had a meeting with a prospect that didn't go well. Point by point, I matched eveɪything the competition offered, but I couldn't get the person to agree to another meeting with me. I don't know what I could have done differently."

If you've ever had a first meeting with a prospect who appeared to meander, that didn't result in a next step—but should have—you're in good company. Just about every salesperson has had the experience of watching a potentially good meeting stray into "thanks but no thanks" territory. Often, we lose control of these meetings because we didn't structure them correctly—or, worse, didn't try to structure them at all!

Slapshot selling is argumentative, "knee-jerk" selling that spends more time batting away objections than it does finding out about meaningful information that illuminates the prospect's objectives and activities. Slapshot selling is inflexible and geared toward regaining the opportunity to talk. Slapshot selling is selling that says, "Please keep your comments to yourself and let me finish my Power-Point show." Slapshot selling is not a particularly efficient way to sell. It's also a poor way to begin a business relationship.

Your True Competition Isn't Who You Think It Is

Let's start our examination of how to structure the first meeting by examining an unspoken component of it: the competition we face.

In our training seminars, we make a habit of asking people who their most important competition is. The answers we get usually sound like one of the following:

- "Our most important competition is Huge Well-Financed Company."
- "Our most important competition is Little Innovative Company."
- "Our most important competition is ourselves."

While all of these answers are interesting, none of them are correct. In fact, the most important competition you face is what the prospect is already doing.

You have to find out what your prospect is doing and how he or she could do it differently. You are a messenger of change—but you can't change what makes sense to the prospect if you don't know what that is!

Again—don't get distracted by what you think the person or organization needs. Ask yourself: If your prospect actually needed to change that status quo, wouldn't he or she have taken action to do so already?

So: What the person is doing right now is your true competitor.

Asking "Do-Based" Questions

As I've mentioned, finding out what we think the person needs probably isn't going to help us much. And we know that our true competition is what the person is already doing.

In fact, finding out what the person we're talking to has done in the past, is doing now, and wants to do in the future will give us the very best opportunity to discuss the ways we may be able to help the prospect meet key goals.

Our primary selling goal must be to find out what the person's trying to achieve now—and learn whether we can help him or her do that better. Learning what's on the list of "Important Things to Accomplish"—and whether we can help turn those objectives into realities—makes much more sense than attempting to impose some predetermined solution based solely on our own preconceptions.

What's the best way to find out what the person is doing? Ask do-based questions. Let's assume we're selling investment management services.

Here's a classic example of a question that focuses on what the person's actually doing right now and illuminates the status quo:

"I'm just curious—What would you have done (to develop an investment portfolio/plan for retirement/save for college) if I hadn't called you?"

This kind of "do-based" questioning doesn't exist in a vacuum. It takes place within an overall sales process. The process has four steps—Opening, Interviewing, Presentation, and Closing—and the goal of any step is always to get to the next step and, ultimately, to step four.

Of the four steps, which do you think should consume the majority of your time?

Please think about this carefully indeed before you proceed any further in this book. Note that in the ideal sale, you should do roughly 75 percent of your work before the presentation.

Do you realize what that means? It means that if we've gathered the right information about what makes sense to the prospect now, our recommendation (or plan) about what should happen next will make sense, too. If it does, our close will be mercifully brief (and very easy).

So—how does all this affect your planning for the initial meeting? Well, during your first meeting, you will aim to move from the opening into the information-gathering step. You will not attempt to deliver a long monologue, and you certainly won't attempt to close the sale!

If we try to "always be closing," we'll be just as inefficient as everyone else. Instead of the model we just saw, our process will look like what most salespeople do, which is this:

There's a big opening—that's the product dump—then there are a few questions that focus on the needs the salesperson assumes exist. The salesperson might ask, "Are you getting X?" The prospect says, "No, we're getting Y." And the salesperson says, "Well, that's okay, because we offer Y, too." Slapshot! The product dump continues—even though the salesperson has no idea what made the prospect choose Y over X, how Y was selected, or whether Z is under consideration as a replacement.

Then there's a big attempt to make a presentation and an even bigger attempt to close. All without enough information!

Avoiding "Slapshot" Selling in the First Meeting

Individual investors, for instance, are often surprised, and a little annoyed to be informed during the first meeting that they need more help with their investment portfolio. And yet that's what most of the people who try to sell them are actually saying: "We already know what you need; we already know what you're getting; we've got something better."

We can't assume we know what the other person's unique aspirations are if we don't ask about them during the first meeting! But how should we ask about those aspirations in a way that will keep the other person from freezing up on us? How, exactly, should we launch the information-gathering phase?

The answer lies in using a flexible questioning and interviewing model. We know that we want to find out what the prospect does. But the questions we pose to uncover that information can't simply be recited one after another. We have to let the prospect's responses affect the direction of the discussion. Otherwise, it's not a great sales meeting—it's an interrogation. News flash: Prospects don't like interrogations.

By contrast, in the best sales meetings, we get to pose "big" questions, and the prospect gets to set the agenda within the area covered by each of those "big" questions. Fortunately, there's a pattern—a roadmap—we can follow to make exactly this kind of discussion happen. We call it the PIPA Sequence. And we'll be examining it in depth in the next chapter. For now, remember this: Slapshot selling—the kind of selling that happens when nervous salespeople try to "take control" of the discussion by firing off memorized questions or reciting product information—is guaranteed to get prospects to tune out.

Strategy #65

Master PIPA—and Learn the Art of Conducting a Great First Meeting

A questioning pattern I call the PIPA sequence can produce spectacular results for you from the very first moments of your initial meeting with the prospect. Let's see how the sequence works at the beginning of a meeting. (Note: The PIPA sequence can be adapted to virtually any point in any conversation, but it's easiest to understand if you apply it to the beginning of any discussion.)

As a matter of social convention, "icebreaker" questions—questions that help you build rapport and a sense of commonality with the other person—are likely to begin your meeting. Bear in mind, though, that even these kinds of questions can be pointed in a direction that illuminates your prospect's unique situation. For instance:

"I'm just curious, how does someone get to be a (Vice President of Widget Reclamation/Senior Data Analyst/CEO/etc.)?"

Once you have completed this small talk portion of your initial meeting, you will be ready to make a seamless transition into the "business" segment of the meeting. The first "P" in the PIPA sequence will help you do just that.

The First "P" in PIPA—Presenting

After the brief get-acquainted portion of the meeting draws to a close (usually indicated by a sizable pause), direct the meeting toward the business at hand by asking something along the following lines:

"Mr. Prospect, would it help if I told you a little bit about our company and what we do?"

By doing this, you are presenting an option—that is to say, implementing the first "P" in the PIPA sequence.

This question—which virtually always yields a yes answer—is not an excuse to execute a product dump.

In the unlikely event that the prospect tells you he or she doesn't want to hear about what you and your company do, but has something else pressing to discuss, simply follow the prospect's lead. The information-gathering phase of the meeting has begun with virtually no effort from you on the transition.

The "I" in PIPA—Interviewing

The "Would it help if I told you a little bit about us" question points us toward a concise, bare-bones statement of our own experience and the company's history. It might sound like this:

"Well, ABC Widget Development is the largest specialized widget manufacturing company in the United States. We've been in business since 1923, and I've been working for the company as a senior account representative since 1997."

We must now immediately pose a question that meets three qualifications:

1. It focuses on what the prospect does.
2. It focuses on some broadly defined area where we have added value for other customers.
3. It is likely to be easy for the prospect to answer.

The moment we pose this "do-focused" question in an area in which we feel we can add value, we are seamlessly making the transition into the second, and most important, part of the PIPA sequence—gathering information. So we would conclude our "little bit about us" statement by saying, "Mr. Prospect, I'm just curious, have you ever worked with a custom widget manufacturer before?"

(A side note: "I'm just curious" and "By the way" are extremely effective phrases for introducing questions.)

Look at the critical transition out of small talk once again.

- Small talk (builds rapport, establishes commonality; may include illuminating questions about the person's past, such as, "How does someone become a . . .?")
- We ask: "Would it help if I told you a little bit about us?" (The prospect will virtually always agree.)
- We deliver a brief commercial. (Two or three sentences should probably be your outer limit.)
- We immediately ask a question that focuses on what the prospect does, addresses an area where we have added value in the past to other customers, and is probably easy for the prospect to answer.

And here's what the transition might sound like in action. Note again that the question must be posed immediately after our brief commercial.

"Well, ABC Widget Development is the largest specialized widget manufacturing company in the United States. We've been in business since 1923, and I've been working for the company as a senior account representative since 1997. I'm just curious, have you ever worked with a specialized widget manufacturer before?"

Strategize Your First Question in the Interviewing Phase

Know the first question you plan to ask after the small talk section concludes!

There is simply no excuse for "winging" the first question in the "I" portion of the PIPA sequence. Let's assume our company offers investment services. On the next page are examples of "do-based" questions that could be a good starting point for our discussion. Each could help you make the transition from "Would it help if I told you a little bit about us?" to gathering information.

- *If the prospect contacted you:* "I'm just curious—what made you decide to call us about investment strategies?"
- *If you contacted the prospect:* "I'm just curious—what were you going to do if I hadn't gotten in touch with you?"
- "I'm just curious—have you ever worked with an investment advisor before?"
- "Really? How did you choose them?"
- "I'm just curious—what kinds of investments have you focused on in the past?"
- "How did they work out for you?"

175

Where Do You Go from There?

Broadly speaking, you want to explore the past, the present, and the future—with "big" questions that focus on how or why. For instance:

- *Past:* "What results did you expect from that approach?" Possible follow-up: "How did you decide whether or not to continue doing that?"
- *Present:* "What are you doing now in this area?" Possible follow-up: "Why did you choose to work with XYZ company?"
- *Future:* "What would you personally like to accomplish in this area?" Possible follow-up: "How will you measure whether or not you're getting closer to that goal?"

Make Sure You Know the Basics

Even though you should never try to impose a predetermined sequence of questions on your prospect, there are certain essential pieces of information you should always try to secure at some point during the first meeting.

Specifically, you should not consider the first meeting a success unless you have recorded, in written form, the following:

- The essentials of the prospect's work history
- The kinds of internal and external customers the prospect must keep happy on a regular basis
- What the prospect is trying to accomplish
- The standards used for previous purchase decisions in your area

A great way to learn the decision-making process in past purchase decisions is to ask, "Why did you decide to do it that way?" or "How did you choose them?"

The Second "P" in PIPA—Present a Next Step Option

Once you have gathered enough information to get a sense of where the relationship should go next, you'll be in a great position to use the second "P" in PIPA. You will present a next step recommendation.

It could sound like this:

"Based on what you've told me today—specifically X, Y, and Z—I think I should put together a preliminary proposal to give you an idea of what we might be able to do for you in this area. Why don't I come back here next Tuesday at two o'clock?"

Always ask for a next step that's easy, logical, and helpful and that's connected to a specific date and time. Make the subject of your conversation when you'll be meeting next, not whether you'll be meeting next. See what happens!

By the way, the second "P" in PIPA also reminds you of "parable selling"—which is an excellent way to use your organization's success stories to position yourself for the next step. This is often (but not always!) a preliminary to presenting a next step option.

Parable selling sounds like this: "It's interesting that you mention XYZ challenge—that's very similar to the situation I faced with my last customer, Tommy Bigshot. What we found was . . . ." You might conclude with: "Why don't I come back here next Tuesday at two o'clock and show you the plan I put together for Bigshot?"

The "A" in PIPA—Agreement That Your Next Step Makes Sense

It's not enough simply to present a next step option. In the "A" portion of the PIPA sequence, you make sure that the other person specifically agrees to the step you have proposed.

Your prospect may agree immediately with the next step you suggest. Then again, he or she may offer a confusing or uncertain response. When this happens, you will want to tactfully but firmly move the issue to the forefront by exploring whether or not what you've suggested makes sense.

The best way to find out about this is simply to ask: "So—do you think it makes sense for us to get together again at this time next week?"

The beauty of this approach is that if it doesn't make sense to the other person, he or she will usually explain why it doesn't!

If the person doesn't provide any information about why the next step you've proposed doesn't make sense, use the "I didn't anticipate that" technique outlined below.

You:	*So—do you think it makes sense for us to get together again next Tuesday at two o'clock?*
Prospect:	*I'd really rather not.*
You:	*I'll be honest—that's a surprise to me. Did I do something wrong?*
Prospect:	*Oh, no—it's nothing you did. The problem's on our end. You see, the thing is…*

Those are the magic words: "The thing is . . . ." Now you're going to hear more critical information. Be sure to take careful note of anything and everything that follows the words "The thing is"! This information is likely to be extremely important.

Use the PIPA sequence. If something goes wrong in the affirmation or agreement step, take responsibility! Be willing to ask, "Did I do something wrong?" Listen carefully for the magic words likely to come your way in response: "The thing is . . . ."

Strategy #66

Review Your Most Important Questions Before the Meeting

Here are just a few of the questions you should consider asking during the all-important information-gathering phase of your meeting. (If memorizing them is difficult, consider writing these—or others—down on your legal pad before you leave for the meeting!)

- "How's business?"
- "What would you have done in such-and-such an area if I hadn't called you?"
- "I'm just curious—what are you trying to make happen here over the next thirty days?"
- "I'm just curious—what do you do here?"
- "How does your company sell its product/service?"
- "How many people work here? Do they report to you?"
- "How many people do you work with who operate out of other locations?"
- "How do you maintain a competitive edge in an industry like this?"
- "How is your organization structured? How many offices/locations do you have?"
- "What are you doing now to grow your business?"
- "What are you doing now to reach out to new customers?"

- "What are you doing now to stay close to your existing customers?"
- "What are you doing now to service your accounts better?"
- "What are you doing now to track what your branch offices are doing on a daily basis?"
- "What are you doing to make it easier for customers to respond to your mailings?"
- "What made you decide to make X a priority right now?"
- "What kinds of new customers are you trying to attract?"
- "Who do you consider to be your biggest competitor? Why?"
- "How do you distinguish yourself from companies like X, Y, and Z in an industry like this?"
- "Is your industry changing? How?"
- "What was the last quarter/year like for you?"
- "Why did you decide to work with ABC Company?"

Whatever questions you ask, you should make a point of reviewing them ahead of time. As I've noted earlier, we tend to fall back on what is most familiar to us. Be sure that what's most familiar to you as you walk in the door to the meeting is the PIPA sequence and the first four or five questions (at least) that you'd like to ask during the course of the meeting.

Know—and practice—the first few questions you plan to ask at the meeting. This is vitally important because you will be in an unfamiliar setting with an unfamiliar person during your initial meeting. That equals stress, and during stressful situations, you will naturally revert to that which is most familiar to you.

Strategy #67

Don't Present Too Early

Is your closing ratio significantly lower than it should be? In all likelihood, the reason is a simple one: You are trying to close *before* you've gathered enough information to make an intelligent recommendation.

Always remember: About three-quarters of your time must be invested in the work that comes *before* the presentation!

Ask yourself: Am I sure I'm talking to the right person? (This is either the decision-maker or the person who can get the decision made for you.) If the answer is no, you are not ready to make a formal presentation.

Ask yourself: Am I sure this plan makes sense, based on what I know this person is actually trying to do? If the answer is no, you are not ready to make a formal presentation.

Ask yourself: Have I discussed all the budget issues with my contact? Does the pricing make sense? Raise the issue yourself—don't wait for the prospect to do so. If the answer is no, you are not ready to make a formal presentation.

Ask yourself: Have I established a realistic timetable? If the implementation or delivery schedule is still theoretical, there's a problem! You are not ready to make a formal presentation.

Ask yourself: Does my contact know I expect to close this sale? If you have any doubt, say something like this: "I'm going to gather everything we've done into a formal proposal for our meeting next Tuesday, and at that point, I don't see any reason why we wouldn't be able to finalize this." See what happens! This is an especially important point. If the contact does not know that you plan to close the sale, then you are definitely not ready to make a formal presentation.

If you're tempted to skip one of the steps outlined in this chapter, consider one more question. What makes more sense—delivering five customized proposals to five prospects who are "playing ball" with you—or delivering twenty-five uncustomized proposals that have little or nothing to do with what people are trying to accomplish?

Most salespeople make presentations before they're ready to. Don't be one of them.

Strategy #68

Verify Your Information

Often, salespeople ask me: "How can I be sure the presentation I make matches what the prospect is actually doing?"

You can't—unless you verify the information you've gathered.

Take a look at the four steps of the selling cycle from the following chart:

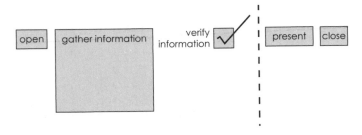

That dotted line between the information-gathering and presentation steps represents a substep—the part of the sale where you verify that the information you think you've gathered really is accurate and complete.

Verifying is a very important concept. You must be willing to be corrected, both to elicit new facts and to verify that you're ready to make the presentation. Some salespeople don't try to verify because they're afraid of making a mistake in front of the prospect. Guess what? If you never get corrected by the people you reach out to, you're not asking the right questions!

The best way to verify your information is by means of a preliminary proposal (also known as an outline). This short document is basically a two- or three-page summary that says, "I am not a proposal." It allows the prospect to give you feedback before you make a formal recommendation.

You want the person to write all over your outline and make all kinds of changes—so you know what kinds of changes to make (and terminology to adopt) before you make a formal recommendation. Once you've used your preliminary proposal to get "righted" during a meeting with the prospect, you can say, "Well, I think we've got everything in place. What I'd like to do is go back and make these changes and then come back here Friday at three o'clock. At that point, we should be able to finalize this and set your delivery dates. Does that make sense?"

When you say that, you'll know exactly where you stand. You'll know for sure whether you've verified the information properly.

Strategy #69

Ask Yourself the Right Questions

In order to conduct an effective meeting with any prospect, you must be confident about the answers to three key questions about your own company.

Question #1

Why do people buy from you? Complete the sentence: "People buy from us because . . . ." Where, specifically, do you add value for your customers? Does your customer base include people who have chosen to work with you for a number of years? Why do they do that? Talk to your sales manager or to colleagues until you get a range of answers. Learn the relevant success stories.

Question #2

What makes you different? Complete the sentence: "The main thing that distinguishes us from/makes us better than other companies that sell what we do is . . . ." Again, work with your colleagues and superiors to develop relevant success stories. Be prepared for the prospect's (fair) question: "Why should I buy from you?"

Question #3

What's more important than price to your customers? Complete the sentence: "Even though we might not be the least expensive option, people choose us because . . . ." These are especially important success stories to learn—and repeat! If you are relying solely on price to win customers, you will not sell deeply or build loyalty in your customer base.

Your answers to each of these questions should lead you to stories or examples of success you or your organization has had with specific clients. Become familiar with those stories.

I realize that these three questions seem simple, and that they take only a few minutes to read silently. May I ask you to take a little extra time right now to complete the three sentences you just read . . . right out loud? If it's possible for you to tape-record your answers to these questions, and review them closely after speaking them into the machine, I urge you to do just that.

This is a very important exercise. If you're like most of the hundreds of thousands of salespeople we've trained, you will find that the simple act of completing these sentences by speaking out loud, without any advance preparation, will motivate you to prepare better, more polished, more carefully practiced answers to these key questions than you may have developed up to this point.

Think about it for a moment. Why *wouldn't* you want to take a moment right now, before proceeding any further in this book, to complete these sentences out loud? Aren't you going to meet prospects that will ask you questions that require you to speak intelligently in each of these areas? Isn't it possible you could meet with one of those prospects within the next twenty-four hours? Why would you make a conscious choice *not* to prepare for those discussions?

Strategy #70

Prepare for the Meeting Properly

How will you prepare for your first face-to-face meeting with a prospect? I believe you should find out the basics about the company. In today's selling environment, there is really no excuse for "cluelessness" about the company's products and services.

I must offer a word of warning here: I'm not one of those sales trainers who advocates that you research a company *to death* before making an in-person visit. Don't overresearch for a first meeting—but do spend a little time gathering the relevant facts. The idea is to make an intelligent investment of your time to figure out a few key facts, not to spend days preparing for every initial meeting. Doing that will only limit the number of meetings you can go on! Give yourself half an hour or so, maybe an hour. Pull up the target company's Web site. Ask yourself: Who are this company's customers? Which of our success stories would be most relevant to this company? What should I be ready to talk about during this meeting?

When you've got the answers to these questions, you should probably move out of "research mode" and think about a different kind of preparation for the meeting.

It is just as important for you to know *what kind of next step* you plan to ask for at the conclusion of this meeting. In other words, what is the outcome you want from this discussion? Specifically: What are you planning to ask for at the conclusion of the appointment? Will you ask for another meeting—at a specific date and time—to review a preliminary proposal? Another meeting—at a specific date and time—to connect with the president of the company? A phone conference—at a specific date and time—to review technical details? A formal commitment to work together on December 15th?

Remember, the next step you ask for must be helpful, logical, and easy for the prospect to agree to. It must also be connected to a specific date and time. And you must ask for it directly before you leave the meeting.

Be sure you plan a primary next step—and a backup next step, just in case the first one doesn't work out.

Strategy #71

Work Your Way up the Ladder

Have you ever found yourself stuck with a 'contact' who knows nothing about the service you're selling. Most of us have. How do we hook up with the real decision-maker?

If you know for certain that your contact cannot make the decision or get the decision made for you, tactfully ask a technical or logistical question your prospect will not be able to answer, but the true decision-maker would be able to answer.

When the person responds, "I don't know," you can say something like this: "Gee, that's actually pretty important. Who would we talk to about that?"

This is an excellent way to move "up the ladder" with your contact.

Your question could sound like this: "How long does the consumer usually have to wait for delivery once the order has been entered into the computer system?"

It's important to verify that the person you're talking to really is the decision-maker. When in doubt, ask a "how" or "why" question, like "Why did you choose that vendor?" or "How did you decide to do that?" These questions will point you toward the real decision-maker.

Ask detailed questions—and try to work with your contact to build alliances that will help you connect with the people who can get them answered.

Don't get misled by titles or organizational charts. Titles can be extremely misleading. A person can have the most impressive title in the world, but have literally no knowledge about the area of activity that title suggests. For instance, a media relations officer may have little or no talent for dealing with editors working under tight deadlines.

Look past the title and the formal organizational structure, and use effective questioning to get your contact to identify the person who has the actual power to make things happen for you. Then try to set a meeting with your contact and that person.

Strategy #72

Get Real—
Strategize Two Weeks in Advance

How much does it really mean when someone tells you they're going to meet with you three, four, or five months from now? Have you ever had such an appointment collapse on you? Of course. We all have.

Let's face it. Projections get less accurate the further into the future they go. Use your calendar as a tool to get as specific as you possibly can about what's going to happen in the near term—preferably before lunch!

What's happening within the next two weeks is what's real. That goes for us and for our prospects.

Get a firm grip on what you can realistically expect to accomplish, create, and earn over the next fourteen calendar days. That's the critical time period, the one that really counts. That's the period you have to spend most of your time focusing on.

By the same token, you should take commitments from other people more seriously when they occupy this two-week window than when they don't. After all, which appointment is more likely to happen—the one I set with you for tomorrow morning at ten o'clock, or the one I set with you for three months from now?

If you were to sit in on the sales meetings we hold in my company, you'd find that the topics of conversation *don't* center on what happened yesterday or last week or last month. We can't affect those events anymore. Why somebody decided to say "no" to us yesterday is about as "closed" a topic as I can imagine. It's done. It has as much relevance to my day as the outcome of the Punic Wars. It may be interesting in some abstract sense when we're planning a discussion with a specific contact in the same industry, but it's not something we spend a lot of time analyzing for its own sake.

Here's something else we don't spend a lot of time analyzing during those meetings: What might happen a month, two months or three months from now that might help someone make a commitment to us. If some event in the far future is particularly important, we'll mark it in our calendars and spend about ten seconds talking about it. But we will not spend any significant portion of the day obsessing about commitments that are scheduled for the distant future.

What we *will* obsess about is how to make commitments happen in the near term—two weeks from today or sooner. That's what we spend our time strategizing, thinking about, brainstorming. That's the chunk of everybody's calendar where the energy is . . . and that, most of the time, is where the revenue comes from.

Strategy #73

Don't Get Distracted by "Yes" Answers

"I just closed a big deal!"

Great!

But let me ask you a question.

Is that the only thing you're counting . . . the deals you've closed, big or small? If so, you're riding for a fall.

Don't just count the "yes" answers! You have to have "no" responses if you want to generate "yes" answers. Anytime a salesperson tells me that a whole week went by without anyone saying "no," I know there's a problem.

Actually, your "no" answers drive the entire sales process. Let's say it takes you, on average, five presentations to secure one sale. And let's say it takes you twenty-one appointments to generate those five presentations. How many "no" answers do you see in that example?

There are nineteen! You really do have to hear those nineteen "no" answers to generate that sale! It's a statistical fact.

So why do we get so hung up on counting the "yes" answers, the sales we close? Why do we just sit there and listen to sales managers when they tell us that we have to hit a certain number of "yes" answers this month? Why don't we take five minutes to translate that "yes" figure we're trying to attain into the number of "no" answers we will need to generate it? In other words, why don't we set a "no" quota for ourselves—and start counting the "no" answers?

Sometimes we get terrified by the word "no," and that's a big problem. The word "no" is not something to fear; it's just part of our process. And it's not just part of our process during the prospecting phase. We have to be willing to hear "no"—that is, to get corrected by our prospects—in order to be correct during the sales process.

Now think about that for a minute. What does that mean? Well, if we assume that we are always right and we already know everything there is to know about the prospect, we're not really learning anything during the information gathering process! At some point, the prospect has to say, "No, that's not really how it is," if we expect to gather or verify any meaningful information.

You really do need a "no" in order to know. If no one ever corrects you or tells you something doesn't work, that means the quality of your information is poor.

Count your "no" answers as well as your "yes" answers. And use the occasional "no" answer to a question or suggestion as an opportunity to get corrected—and verify your information.

Strategy #74

Never Walk Away Without Asking for Some Kind of Action

When I make this point during training programs, sometimes salespeople tell me they are afraid of coming across as being too bossy. What they really mean is that they are afraid to ask politely and clearly for a next step. That's not bossy. That's professional. That's what salespeople do.

You have to ask the other person to do something. Otherwise you have no idea who's actually a prospect and who isn't. So ask! Ask them to schedule a meeting, take a call, meet with your boss—anything!

For instance: How many hundreds of times have you heard someone say over the phone, "Just send me some information." We suggest that salespeople say, "I prefer not to send information—let's just get together instead. How's Tuesday at two o'clock?" That's asking the prospect to do something. Recently, someone we were training was a little bit skeptical about this approach. But he agreed to try it. He picked up the phone. His contact said, "Send me some information." Without really thinking, he said, "Gee, I really prefer not to do that. Let's get together instead. How's Tuesday at two o'clock?"

Because that's what his trainer had said during training—Tuesday at two o'clock.

The contact thought for a minute and said, "Okay. Tuesday at two o'clock it is." Well, the salesperson was not expecting that response. He had to say, "Hold it. Tuesday at two o'clock? I'm really sorry, I can't. I'm busy."

He had to do a little scrambling to secure that appointment—but at least he proved to himself how effective it is to ask the person to do something!

Strategy #75

Never Make a Presentation You Don't Think Will Close

Here's an example of the kind of conversation with a salesperson that drives me crazy.

I ask, "When are you going back?"

The salesperson says, "Tuesday."

I ask, "What are you doing Tuesday?"

The salesperson says, "I'm going to ask for the business."

I say, "Okay—what do you think is going to happen when you ask for the deal? Do you think you're going to close the deal?"

The salesperson thinks for a minute and says, "Well, I don't know. Actually, I don't really think they're ready yet. We'll see what happens Tuesday, but probably not."

Have you ever said anything close to "We'll see what happens Tuesday, but probably not" about a presentation you were about to make? Let me tell you something. That is a recipe for disaster. And by disaster, I mean you spending a week and a half putting together a proposal for someone who hasn't told you what will really make enough sense for him to write a check that your company can put in its bank account. By disaster I mean *you are wasting time that you could have spent building up a deal somewhere else.*

The whole idea behind a recommendation, presentation, or plan is that you honestly think you have found a match. You honestly believe you can help the person do what he or she does better. Wouldn't it be nice to know whether or not the prospect is thinking along the same lines as you are? So what's wrong with asking that? "Hey, you know what, I think there's a match here . . . Based on what you're telling me, I'm thinking the next thing we ought to do together is . . . (fill in the blank!)."

Throughout the sales process, you have to make sure *everything* you're proposing, step by step, really does make sense to the other person. You have to make sure the other person *knows what you plan to do* as a next step. And if the prospect doesn't know what you plan to do next, don't try to do it! That means the other person must know you plan to come back and ask more questions. Or meet with the prospect's boss. Or deliver a preliminary proposal. Or give your formal plan and ask for the business.

When in doubt, say what you plan to do next and see what happens. ("You know, when I come back here next Tuesday, once I address these customization issues you've raised, I'm thinking we're going to be ready to go for a training program in March. What do you think?")

Strategy #76

Always Have a Backup Plan

What will you do if the competition calls your number-one prospect?
What will you do if the meeting doesn't go the way you want it to?
What will you do if your contact at your most important customer moves to another company?
What will you do if your number-one product is obsolete tomorrow morning?

Never stop asking yourself, "What do I do if something goes wrong here?" Ask yourself, "What could make this sale go wrong?" Ask yourself, "What could happen to throw my income projection off—and what can I do to hit my goals anyway?"

Don't just rely on the best-case scenario. Play your scenarios forward. Play your scenarios backward. Figure out your backup plan.

Let's say you've got a prospect who looks good now. Ask yourself, "What does my income picture look like if that prospect falls through the cracks?" It happens!

What's your plan?

Develop a fallback position for your prospect base as a whole by making sure you have enough prospects and enough first appointments. Develop a fallback plan by figuring out a second reason for coming back for another meeting—just in case the first one doesn't work out. You should also develop a fallback plan for your four or five most important customers. If they're only purchasing one thing from you, what else can you present to them? How can you deepen the relationship? How many people within the company are you now in contact with? How can you expand that number? Is there any way for you to gain access to the senior manager, CEO, or company founder? By building a relationship with more (and more influential) people within the account, you maximize your own personal visibility and accountability—and you improve your chances of retaining the account if there's a problem somewhere along the line.

Strategy #77

Never Kid Yourself

Here are six common bits of self-deception that have short-circuited countless sales careers. Don't let them short-circuit yours.

#1. "That's a good prospect."

As you've learned in this book, the only true prospect is someone who commits specifically to work through the sales process with you—by committing to a clear date and time. Anybody else is an opportunity you may want to turn into a prospect. Simply wanting to sell to someone or doing research on a company is not enough! You should maintain a minimum number of active prospects at all times. (What that number is, of course, depends on your own selling cycle and income goals, but you could do worse than to start with twenty prospects and adjust from there based on your own experience.)

#2. "I have enough prospects for now."

At my company, we've trained hundreds of thousands of salespeople over the years. The vast majority of them have fewer active prospects than they think—and they only learn the truth when they hit a fallow period. Unfortunately, it usually takes them weeks or months to build the base of new prospects back up to an optimal level. That's usually a painful period in terms of personal income. It doesn't have to be, though. Prospect daily—and be sure you hit daily targets that support your sales goals.

#3. "That meeting went pretty well."

Did it? If the person didn't agree to meet or speak with you at a specific date and time, it didn't really go well at all!

#4. "I can make this person do what I want to do."

There is nothing you can do to make someone do something he or she does not believe to be in his or her best interests. The key to success in sales lies not in interpersonal manipulation but in getting in front of enough people and asking enough intelligent questions to get a critical percentage of them to act when you make a recommendation based on what you've heard. Thousands of years ago, Lao-tzu wrote in the *Tao Te Ching* that "Gentleness overcomes rigidity." In terms of selling in the twenty-first century, a good translation might be, "You only get to lead after you've demonstrated, by asking and listening, that you are focused on helping the people do what they do better."

#5. "I should be able to close this."

The use of conditional language ("should," "ought," "might") in reference to accounts that you hope to close should be a tip-off that there's a problem somewhere. Why is there any doubt? Does the person know you intend to close the sale? If the prospect doesn't want the sale to happen as much as you do, don't count on it!

#6. "I've got this job down."

Even the most seasoned, most experienced person can go from hero to zero with alarming speed in today's economy. How? By neglecting personal and professional development. Sales is the kind of job you never really "get down." Keep learning. Keep growing. Keep asking, "How can I do this better?" Keep listening to the answers you hear.

Strategy #78

Take Immediate Action

Early on in our relationship with a prospect, we're not the highest thing on his or her priority list. The information we get is better and the commitments we receive are more meaningful as the relationship progresses and deepens. But at the outset of our business relationship, we don't really know what the other person has in mind. We don't know whether that person will get to talk to the other people in the organization who must sign off on our ideas. We don't know whether the prospect will even read our proposal. We need every advantage we can get. Most salespeople are not quick enough to act on what I consider to be the basic responsibility of good sales work: committing oneself to move the process forward, and not relying on others to do so.

In selling, you need to be fast. You need to take responsibility for sizing up the best ways to move the sales cycle forward, and you need to act quickly.

I got a telephone call a number of years ago from a woman who wanted to buy ten copies of my *Cold Calling Techniques (That Really Work!)* book. It happened to be 10:30 at night on a Friday when she called; I was in the office, working late, so I answered the phone.

When I heard that she wanted to order the ten books, I asked myself, "What can I do to move this relationship forward right now?"

So I asked, "What is it you're trying to accomplish? How are you planning to use the books?" To which she said, "I work for a major oil company here in Virginia, and what we're trying to do is get our ten distributors to make more phone calls, and if we do that, we're going to be more effective in our sales." I said to her, "I've got an idea. I'll be in Virginia this coming Tuesday. Why don't we get together?" She said, "You'll come here?" I said, "Absolutely!"

The fact of the matter is that my quick action to move the relationship forward led to a $250,000 sale! All this because I chose to take immediate action to find out more about the person, to deepen the relationship, to move the process forward then and there.

Most salespeople don't do that. In fact, most salespeople are busy trying to figure out how they can avoid having to go on an appointment. They figure maybe they can cut a few corners. My philosophy—and the philosophy of the superior salespeople I've worked with over the years—is very different. Take action, and do it now. Get an answer—positive or negative—quickly, and then move on. Reinforce a good meeting now, not next week. Follow up a promising lead now, not "someday."

For example, recently one of my sales managers ripped out an ad in *BusinessWeek* for a credit corporation and passed it on to a salesperson. The rep made no call on that ad for three weeks. My sales manager, slightly peeved, "repossessed" the ad and called the next day. He got an appointment instantly. We eventually got the business from that ad—but we could have gotten it three weeks earlier than we did. (And that salesperson could have earned a commission!)

Successful salespeople are always thinking about how they can move things forward. They realize that in order to change the status quo, it's usually necessary to act quickly.

Don't overanalyze a situation. Act immediately. Go when the prospect says to go. But also be realistic about what you're going there for—and don't be shy about following up immediately after your appointment, either on paper or by phone. When in doubt, take action! Do something that moves the relationship forward!

Strategy #79

Take Quiet Time to Think

Most salespeople, I've found, don't give themselves enough time to think. The successful salespeople I've worked with have usually found ways to build quiet time into their work week—time they use to reflect on where they are, what they're doing, and where they should be going.

It's usually a good idea to find a special place where you can think about your work without being questioned or disturbed. (A salesperson I know recently tried to sit quietly in his own living room so he could think about the challenges he faced in the upcoming week, but family members, unused to his silence, kept walking in and asking him what was the matter with him!)

I love to work on Saturdays, when no one else is in the office, just so I can think. I come in the office, usually about ten o'clock, do some of the paperwork that I have to do, and then think for the next two hours. I don't try to write, necessarily. I go through some papers, review to-do lists, and look at schedules—all of which triggers my imagination and lets me reflect on the work that I'm doing. But I don't interact with other people, and I don't talk. I keep a pad of paper handy so I can write down notes to myself. You deserve some kind of quiet time, too.

Superior salespeople make a habit of analyzing exactly what they are trying to accomplish. They take the time to immerse themselves in their "game plan," reflect on that plan, and look at it from lots of different angles. They ask themselves:

- What am I doing now that's working?
- Why is it working?
- What am I doing now that's not working?
- Why isn't it working?
- What could I be doing differently?

Sales is hard work. It requires persistence, and you do have to make sure you follow through. But you also have to understand what you're trying to accomplish in the first place. Superior salespeople are not robots. They're involved in their own careers, and they make their own decisions. They follow the marketplace trends that affect them. And they make adjustments. Use your quiet time to ask yourself "what's working" questions along the lines of the ones outlined above.

Ask yourself what you can do that will make it easier to achieve your goals. How can you change your selling routine for the better? If you usually make your prospecting calls in the afternoon, what would happen if you made them in the morning, while you're still fresh and enthusiastic? If you usually call the benefits administrator, what would happen if you called the president of the company? What other contacts can you reach out to within your existing accounts?

That last question is a great example of how thinking through new approaches on a regular basis can really boost your income. Most salespeople sell on the horizontal. That is, they sell to the person who bought from them initially. They never really think out ways in which they can escalate their totals by moving on to another person. So they end up selling to the same person who bought a limited amount from them in the first place, and who may lack the authority to buy any additional amount. Such an "upgrade" of your contacts within an organization may require careful planning—but that's what quiet thinking time is for!

We have to take the time to think through our own sales objectives. We also have to take the time to think through the past, present, and future of our prospects and customers. By spending some quiet time with yourself every week (at least), you'll be in a better position to do more things that work, and stop doing things that don't.

Strategy #80

Seize Opportunities

Many salespeople see opportunity. Few salespeople seize opportunity. Seizing the opportunity means employing all the techniques possible. It means doing things most other salespeople don't. Superior salespeople identify opportunities quickly and effectively, and then they use all their resources to turn potential success into sales dollars.

Seizing the opportunity means taking full advantage of each new situation as it presents itself. And, paradoxically, seizing the opportunity means being able to keep from getting distracted with the idea of closing the sale.

Successful salespeople realize that the phrase "closing a sale" is something of a misnomer. What you're really after is to get people to buy from you—that is, to use your products. Therefore, you have to develop a plan, also called a proposal, which will show the prospect why he or she should use your product or service. But here's the tricky part: that proposal has to be customized.

The most effective salespeople I know don't use boilerplate proposals. They seize the opportunity to improve the relationship by getting the prospect to develop the proposal with them, step by step, based on the information they've gathered during the interview.

Here's one great way to seize the opportunity: transform the situation when you are asked to "deliver a presentation" to a group. Instead, set up a flipchart, give a brief overview of what you want to do, and then let the group "write" the proposal for you. Ask questions like, "What are you trying to get accomplished in X area?" Then write down everything—and I mean everything—you hear in response on that flipchart. Use your notes to develop a preliminary proposal, one the committee can pick apart before you finalize things for your formal proposal. That's a great way to seize opportunity.

Don't wait for the sale to fall into your lap. Don't assume you know the answers. Don't assume that you have to deliver a boilerplate slide show just because that's what everyone else is doing. Change the pattern! Ask the questions! Write down the answers! Find out exactly what makes this opportunity unique! And seize it!

Strategy #81

Be Punctual

Not long ago, a salesperson came in to see me. He was fifteen minutes late. He didn't understand why I was a little bit annoyed at his tardiness. But think about it. Did you ever go to a doctor or dentist who made you wait for twenty minutes—after you'd rushed to get to his office on time? There you are taking a taxicab or driving at breakneck speed in order to get to the dentist for your 4:00 appointment—only to have to spend twenty minutes waiting? That's pretty aggravating, isn't it? My question is: Why on earth should we subject our prospects to those experiences?

A salesperson must be punctual. Period. When a prospect blocks out time to meet with you, you have to move heaven and earth to make the meeting happen at the time you've committed to—and that usually means planning on making your way into the office five or ten minutes before the appointed time.

Treat your own time, and the time of your prospect, with respect. You can do this by:

- Scheduling "hard" appointments ("Yes, I'll meet you at 10:00 on Tuesday morning) around nearby "soft" appointments ("I think we can meet at 1:00, but you'll have to call me to confirm the meeting in the morning"). That way, if your soft appointment falls through, you haven't made a trip for no reason.

- Use your off time (say, 5:30–6:00 P.M.) to compose thank-you letters.

- On those rare occasions when you can't make a scheduled meeting as the result of a dire emergency, call ahead and explain the problem—or try to arrange for a manager or colleague to stand in for you.

- Buy yourself a day planner or other personal scheduling aid and use it each and every day.

- Never overbook yourself. If you can't make a certain date and time, say so up front and schedule your appointment for a date that's not as full.

- Remember who's in charge. If your client needs a few extra minutes to resolve an office crisis before sitting down to meet with you, don't stew about it in the waiting room! Your frustration will show, and will negatively affect the emotional atmosphere of the meeting.

Strategy #82

Return Calls Within Twenty-Four Hours

I have a policy in my office that none of my calls are screened—and I encourage the salespeople who work for me to follow my example. For the most part, the calls simply come to me: "Mary Smith on line two." As a result, I talk to just about everybody when I'm in the office. I also have all my messages forwarded to me when I'm out of the office. And I return calls within twenty-four hours.

Now, perhaps there's a case to be made that I talk to a lot of people who I don't need to speak to. And yet, every once in a while, there are people who call me because they want my organization to conduct a program for them, people whose names are unfamiliar to me. How can I risk skipping a message or dodging a call when there's a chance that business could be attached to it?

My philosophy, and the philosophy of the most successful salespeople I know, is that you can never afford not to call somebody back—no matter how trivial the call may seem. There's a reason that somebody has called you. The reason may not be what you think it is, but there's a reason why someone has called. Therefore, you really should call that person back, if only to find out what the objective of the call was, and you should find a way to do so within a single business day.

I could give you hundreds of stories of people who have called me up just because they read one of my books and had something (positive or negative) to say about it. And inevitably, when I'm on the phone with someone like that I simply say, "Gee, I'm curious— what do you do for a living?" And in the ensuing conversation I find out more about their businesses, and in some cases, I get opportunities to sell. The point is that by making a commitment to call people back, you find out more about them, and you may uncover new opportunities.

So make the call—while you still have the note, while the question or problem is fresh in your caller's mind, while the "urgency factor" is still working on your side, while you still have a chance to make a good impression. Make no mistake: Returning calls courteously and promptly is probably the single best way to distinguish yourself from the competition in this fast-paced economy of ours. Whether you sell sales training or long-distance services or insurance, you want to send the right message: "You're important to me, so important that I'm going to return your call, or see to it that someone else does within twenty-four hours."

Many years ago, I made a sales call to a major communications and technology firm. There in the conference room was a huge poster of the comedian Bob Newhart. (You may remember that his early routines were based on premises that involved his talking to people on the phone.) Beneath this huge poster is a caption: "Return your calls, even internal calls, within twenty-four hours."

Apparently this huge company had a problem: Their people weren't returning telephone calls! Hence the awareness campaign. That poster inspired the standard we follow at D.E.I.: Respond to each and every incoming message—and, yes, that includes e-mail messages—within one business day.

Strategy #83

See Everyone at Least Once

I feel very strongly about this principle. I believe salespeople should meet, at least once, with everybody who calls in and is willing to set an appointment. By the same token, I also believe that there's no greater time-management sin than continuing to meet, or perpetually attempting to schedule new appointments, with "prospects" who don't represent realistic opportunities for future business.

But first-time appointments? I will make every possible effort to schedule those with anyone who calls me or whom I call—and yes that includes salespeople who call trying to sell me something.

You never know where a meeting is going to lead. As an average, every person knows 250 other people. At the very least, agreeing to first-time meetings, whether they're with prospects, competitors, or salespeople, puts you in touch with a new network of people.

Recently, a sales rep for an investment firm called me up to ask for an appointment. Not having any reason not to see the person, I said, "Of course I'll see you." Not only did I have the opportunity to hear the person's presentation (a big plus, since evaluating the work of other salespeople is one of my favorite pastimes), but I actually became interested in what this fellow's company had to offer. As it turned out, I became a customer.

At the end of this meeting, I asked the rep, "How did you learn to sell this way? Just how did it come about?" And he started describing a situation with his manager. His manager held weekly meetings, attempting to motivate and train his salespeople.

I called the manager and, without mentioning that I had recently done business with his company, asked for an appointment. The manager was more than happy to meet with me—and I eventually landed a new client for my company!

You really never know who's going to come into your world, and you have to be amenable to the idea of meeting new people. Meet as many people as you possibly can. Commit to a first meeting. Just be sure the person knows what you do for a living and knows who you do it for.

I don't know why so many salespeople are frightened to reach out and meet new contacts, but I do know that those who retain this fear don't move on to become superstars.

Now it's true, not everybody you're going to see is going to buy from you. Yet it's also true that, to become truly successful in sales, you have to develop an inquisitiveness about seeing people, meeting people, and understanding what's happening in their lives and in their businesses. You can't be afraid to ask, "Hey, why don't we get together Tuesday at 10:00 A.M.?" And you can't be afraid to say, "Sure, I'm free for lunch on Thursday. Come on in. Let's chat."

What's the worst thing that can happen? You can identify a mismatch. That's really no problem. You just move on. But at the very least you've passed along a business card, learned a little more about the world you live in, and maybe, just maybe, picked up some more information about the ways you should—and shouldn't—try to sell to other people. And you might just have a good time in the process.

Strategy #84

Know When to Retreat

Recently, I was in California working with one of my sales representatives. We were talking about a prospect who he had been working with for the last four or five weeks. He'd gone to the prospect's office, gotten his information together, and made a good, solid proposal. In fact, his proposal was so good that I thought it really did make sense for us to do business with this company.

When I accompanied my rep on his third sales call to this company, I said to the prospect, "Bob, I really believe this proposal makes sense and we should go ahead." Bob was extremely interested in what we had to say, and he, too, felt it made sense. The only problem was that there were a couple of minor issues that still needed to be resolved; we would have to return with a more specific, revised proposal.

Things looked good until my sales rep called again the following week and could not get Bob on the phone. After three attempts to get a return call, he called me up and said, "Steve, can you call Bob and see if you can get him on the phone?" I called once but didn't get him on the phone. Eventually, it became quite obvious that Bob did not want to return our calls. And the sale, for now, was dead.

So what's the lesson to be learned? There are times when it makes sense to retreat and not waste any more of your time pursuing a prospect. (In this case, that time came around the fifth unreturned call, although an argument could be made that it could even have come a little sooner.) Sometimes you're just not the right person to make the sale, and sometimes it's not going to happen, no matter how good you think you are and no matter how much sense it seems to make for you and the prospect to do business together. Sometimes you do the very best you can and it's pretty darned good, and things still don't work out.

Unfortunately, a lot of salespeople continue making calls well after this point of honorable retreat has passed. They continue going back to the same prospect week after week. I was up in Canada not long ago, working with a major telecommunications company there, and I noticed that the pages of most of the salespeople's notebooks were dog-eared. Each page had a profile on a different prospect. These reps were simply calling the same prospects—prospects that had repeatedly rejected them—over and over again! Where on earth, I thought to myself, was the new business supposed to come from?

I've talked to many salespeople who tell me that they make 100 cold calls a day. In fact, what they do is call ten familiar people ten times a day. That may add up to 100 somethings, but it's not 100 cold calls in my book. I once ran into a sales rep who swore up and down that she had called someone 437 times in a vain attempt to get an appointment. I don't know whether I believe the part about the number of calls, but I do believe she never managed to schedule the appointment. The poor prospect must have dreaded the idea of developing a long-term business relationship with this person!

It's important to understand that some prospects will say "no" to you by never saying anything. You have to realize when you're getting that message and be willing to move on. In Bob's case, he'd really left us a message even though he hadn't left us a message.

That is, his refusal to return the calls really was telling us something. He wasn't interested in doing business with us. So what's the point of going back and calling him over and over again? That's a game that far too often turns into an adversarial situation. The unspoken message: "You'd better call me back quick—because I want an explanation about why you haven't returned my last seventeen phone calls." How likely is it that you'll want to launch a business relationship that starts out like that?

In some cases, there really is nothing we can do to turn the situation around. Not many sales trainers will admit this openly, but in the real world, it's quite common to run into situations where your best and most appropriate response is to leave the prospect alone and spend your time in a more efficient way (i.e., call someone else). When you run into someone like Bob—someone who decides to simply drop out of the relationship—don't play ego games. Let it go. Forget it. Pass. Leave it alone. Move on.

Sometimes the chemistry simply doesn't click; sometimes you have no control whatsoever over the reason someone decides not to do business with you. Maybe you're too tall or too short or too redheaded or too something else that turns this person off. Find someone else to talk to—don't take it personally. You can't make a trusting business relationship happen by sheer force of will—it's a consensual dance between two people. If one of the people doesn't feel right about the way something's going, there's no point in pressing the matter.

Years ago, my two daughters had two gerbils. Both gerbils ran around in that little wheel that we got them. At night they would go around and around and around, and they were exhausted during the day even though they actually had gone no place at night. We call that "gerbil salesmanship." I've talked about that kind of sales work in many of my seminars. Some salespeople go around and around and around, never getting ahead. All they manage to do is tick off someone—someone who might have represented a prospect at some point in the future, but now won't, because of the "curse of the gerbil."

It happens to everyone. Major sales seem within our reach and then, for unfathomable reasons, they collapse. If you know when to walk away, you still have the chance to do business with that prospect at some point in the future. If you don't know when to walk away, but insist on badgering your prospect until he gets anxious when he hears your name or your company's name, then beware: You've just inherited the curse of the gerbil. This prospect, and this company, will, in all likelihood, never do business with you.

Think in the long term, and remember that "retreat" doesn't mean "defeat." Twelve years ago, I tried to sell our sales training services to a major New York bank, but the bank president looked me in the eye and said to me, "Look, let me put this as plainly as I can: We'll never hire people like you. We don't want to have the kind of culture you represent. Thank you very much." Talk about a crash and burn! And yet, about three months ago, I conducted the first of a series of training programs for that bank.

Time passes, things change. Don't be too concerned about temporary setbacks. Keep your eyes on your job, don't play head games, do your best, and you will eventually get business from a lot of the people who once didn't give you business. I promise. In the meantime, learn when to back off.

There's a difference between being persistent and being obnoxiously persistent. Sometimes the best and most effective brand of persistence is that which allows you to disengage for a while and see what happens. Make sure you're on the right side of the line—and make sure you don't waste your precious time on prospects who've already taken themselves out of your cycle.

We will all lose battles. The objective is not to avoid losing a single battle, but to win the war. When it's time to retreat, pick up the phone and start prospecting so you can build a business relationship with someone new.

Strategy #85

Know How to Develop Interdependent Relationships

Successful salespeople realize that their work is about relationships.

There are actually four levels that each of us go through when we're selling. The first level is that of the seller, meaning that we're (for lack of a better word) peddlers. Now that's the lowest common denominator that I can think of when I describe a salesperson: a peddler. We come in and we only talk about dollars (or instant delivery, or some other topic of instant and immediate interest to the prospect). We close the sale on one factor that is of deep interest to our customers. There's only the vaguest hint of a real relationship with the customer. Everything is set up for the short term. We don't really expect this connection to last for long. We may have the best price—for now—but we're incredibly vulnerable to competitors, and the moment a better price (or a faster turnaround or a better service plan) comes along, we're almost certainly going to lose a customer.

The second level is that of the supplier. A supplier is typically somebody from whom a customer buys something on an ongoing basis. We're still vulnerable to shifts, but perhaps not as vulnerable as we were when we were a seller. We've got a little bit more information about what the prospect is doing, but we still don't know all that much about his or her business.

The third level is that of the vendor. The name "vendor" implies loyalty, trust, and a deepening relationship. The aspect of trust is important: the customer trusts you, you understand the customer. You've come through on a number of different levels. You're not going to wake up to learn that you're no longer selling to this customer. If there's a sudden strategic change, you're going to have some advance warning, and probably a chance to establish the relationship on a new footing.

Most salespeople tend to be either sellers or suppliers. A minority work their way into the third level, that of the vendor. But highly successful salespeople move on to a fourth level. They become partners.

Highly successful salespeople work for months and years to develop relationships with customers that are interdependent and mutually beneficial—not unlike a marriage. As in any good marriage, both partners need each other, and there's a shared planning process. If you track down as much information as you can about the company you're selling to, if you learn as much about its challenges and goals as some of the senior people at that company, if you consistently develop ways that help these people do what they do better, if your contacts routinely request your input before making major strategic decisions, then you're a lot more than just a salesperson. You're a partner.

For the last twelve years I've been working with a major company, and every single November we plan out the next year's activity—not just what kind of seminars I'm planning to offer, but how those seminars and training sessions can best support the company's most important emerging objectives.

That's partnership. That's the ideal situation. That's the payoff for asking the right questions over a long period of time—and working with your contact to find the best ways to help his or her organization do what it does better. Your goal is a relationship in which you and the customer depend on each other in a partnership relationship.

Sales is fundamentally dependent upon other people, but it's only when we reach the partnership phase that we realize the many benefits of this dependency. There are a million things you can do by yourself, but there is really nothing about success in sales that can be traced to anything you do by yourself. Sales is a dependent activity. The better you work with and interact with other people, the more successful you're likely to be.

Sales, then, is all about relationships. Superior salespeople learn how to build those relationships properly.

A lot of salespeople confuse relationships with time. Don't be one of them. The fact that I spend a lot of time with you does not mean that I have a great relationship with you. (You could be, for instance, looking for a way to justify your presence on the staff; maybe scheduling lots of meetings with lots of salespeople is the way you accomplish that. I've met plenty of people who fall into this category!)

Relationships aren't static; they're interdependent and dynamic. Having a real relationship with a prospect or customer is the same thing as being part of the planning process...and moving toward that partnership role.

Strategy #86

Know When Not to Be Dependent

Here, I'm talking about avoiding the trap of believing that someone other than you can assume responsibility for building and maintaining relationships with your prospects and customers.

I'm often criticized because I believe that a sales manager's only function in life is to make sure that the salespeople on his staff get paid—that is, to see that they get their full commission and, occasionally, to accompany them on sales calls. (The sales manager's presence can serve as a signal of how important the prospect is to your organization.) Sales managers do not, however, show up in the morning to make sales—and despite what some in your organization may think, they cannot motivate the salespeople who report to them.

As a salesperson, both of those jobs, selling to prospects and customers and keeping yourself motivated, are yours and yours alone. Depending on sales managers to establish final terms with the prospect is not the kind of help for which you should appeal. If you're not taking responsibility for the relationship with your customer, then you're not doing your job as a salesperson. And if you look to someone else to motivate you on a daily basis, then you're definitely not doing your job as a salesperson.

Fortunately, the very fact that you're reading these words means that you're already ahead of the game when it comes to taking responsibility for key aspects of your job as a salesperson. Ninety percent of all salespeople in the United States fail to read a sales book during the course of a given year!

How can you continue the good work and take full responsibility for your own motivation and your relationships with your prospects and customers? Here are some of the steps the highly successful salespeople I've worked with have taken:

- Get organized. Set up a priority list that allows you to focus on the most important objectives each day, and review that list regularly.
- Focus on the best prospects first. Divide your active prospects into A, B, and C categories—and make sure you spend the majority of your time with the prospects who represent the "best bets." Don't simply call your list in the order in which the cards happen to be stacked on the desk!
- Develop a regular prospecting routine. Many salespeople don't have enough prospects in the pipeline at any given moment to account for the natural erosion of prospects (which occurs any time you sell something!). Instead, they prospect in a hit-or-miss fashion, when they can't think of anything better to do. Successful salespeople, on the other hand, prospect for new business daily—typically for at least an hour a day.
- Write letters and make calls. Take responsibility for relationships—thank the new people on your calendar for taking the time to see you, and thank current customers for their business. In addition, you should occasionally call or drop a line to contacts you haven't heard from in a while.

Don't expect the higher-ups in your organization to let your customers know how much their business means to you. Do it yourself! You won't regret doing so. Recently, I called thirty-five of the people who had played a major role in giving my company business in the last quarter. I simply thanked them for the business. Out of those thirty-five calls, nine people called me back specifically to give me additional business for the next quarter! That's a high-impact calling campaign if there ever was one.

Know when not to be dependent! You can't expect anyone else to manage your sales career for you. You have to do it yourself, one day at a time.

Strategy #87

Consider Yourself to Be a Messenger of Change

As I've mentioned, there's a point in my seminars when I ask sales-people, "Who's your number-one competitor?" Of course, they name every company they can think of that's offering a similar prod-uct or service. And they're all wrong. The number-one competitor every single company faces is the status quo. What the prospect is already doing is your competition! As we've seen, the key objective of selling is asking people what they do, how they do it, when they do it, where they do it, who they do it with, and why they're doing it that way. And then our job is to help them do it better. But in order to help them do it better we actually have to become messengers of positive change. Successful salespeople are prepared to do that, day in and day out.

In order to be successful at selling, you're going to have to get someone to change what he's doing now, to work with you instead of following the path of least resistance. Are you ready for that?

How do you pull something like that off? First and foremost, you have to know your own product or service very well. (In other words, you have to be comfortable actually using it, just as a customer would.) Number two, you have to be convinced, deep down, no kidding, that your product will, in fact, help people. And finally, you have to be versatile enough to adapt your product or service to whatever it is the customer is trying to do. This assumes, of course, that you're willing and able to listen to the customer long enough to find out what he or she is trying to do!

Not long ago, I was teaching a course in a high school about sales. (Yes, believe it or not, there are people in high school who are interested in careers in sales!) As part of our giveback to the community, we do work with high school students in New York City; at the conclusion of one class, I was asking the students to tell me what they'd picked up from this initial discussion that we'd had about sales. One young man raised his hand and said to me, "Mr. Schiffman, the one thing that I've learned today is that you aren't as important as what the customer is all about; you have to say to yourself, 'The customer is really more important to me than anything else.' And what it is they want to do, what they are trying to accomplish, and how they want to do that is much more important than your product or anything that you have to say."

He was absolutely right. A superior salesperson has to accept that. There's no lecturing prospects or customers, no reading from brochures, no memorized monologues. None of that is as important as asking, "Hey, what are you trying to get accomplished here?" and then listening for the answer that comes our way. Once we hear that answer, once we can respond intelligently with suggestions based on our own product knowledge, then we're in a position to help bring about positive change. Not beforehand!

Strategy #88

Prioritize, Don't Apologize

It's been said that 90 percent of the things we worry about never happen, and that 5 percent of the things we worry about are things that we can't do anything about. That leaves us spending 95 percent of our worrying time focusing on the wrong things!

Superior salespeople know how to distinguish important or critical problems from mundane ones. I had someone tell me the other day that she was trying to make a sale that she'd been working on for nearly three months. The sale was worth about $50 a month. She had gone back seven times to see this individual. Other prospects on her list represented roughly eight to ten times as much money as this one did.

I asked her, "Why are you doing that? Why are you going back to talk to this person?" She said, "Well, Steve, it really isn't the sale any more, it's the challenge. It's the challenge of making the sale."

That kind of challenge is too expensive!

Many, many salespeople worry about the wrong things. "What if the person says this, or what if the person says that?" Who cares? Make the call and see what happens. If you've been selling for a month or more, you've made enough sales calls in your career to realize that they're not all that different from one another.

Plenty of salespeople get so worked up about what might happen during a sales call or an appointment that they overprepare—and then get completely flummoxed when the prospect or customer doesn't follow the script! Then there are salespeople who get so terrified of their encounters with a customer or prospect whom they go to great lengths to "make contact" with—for instance, by leaving messages—but would really prefer not to interact with the prospect at all!

Why, you ask yourself, would anybody bother to do that? I don't have the answer, but I will tell you that any number of salespeople will go through some amazing routines to reach out to prospects they don't really want to talk to. If that's not a waste of time, I don't know what is. Recently I had someone come into my office, and after sitting and discussing with me what he wanted to sell me, he said, "Mr. Schiffman, what I would like to do is prepare a proposal for you. But I don't want to take your time. I'll just drop it off and you can give me a call." Those were his actual words.

He was basically apologizing for being a salesperson.

I stared at him and said, "Why would you want to do that? Why would you want to go to the trouble of preparing a proposal specifically for me and then drop it off and let me make the decision of whether to make the next call—which I may or may not do? What if I have questions about the proposal?" He said, "Well, Mr. Schiffman, you're busy and I don't want to interrupt what you do."

Well, that's precisely what you're doing when you're a salesperson. You're interrupting what I do because you feel that you can help me do what I do better. You can do that only by setting priorities, listening to me talk about my operation, and, eventually, suggesting what I ought to do next!

Superior salespeople don't apologize for that process, or fret endlessly about its possible ramifications. They know when they stand a good chance of adding value to someone's day and when they don't. They don't worry about things they can't control. They simply make the best evaluations they can, and then act accordingly.

Strategy #89

Notice What's Around You

Recently I did a training program with a company in Los Angeles. Part of my presentation involved challenging the sales reps to find new opportunities for business—material for prospecting that no one in the organization had taken advantage of up to that point. Most of the salespeople I was working with were skeptical. "We've already pretty much done it all," they told me. "There are no new companies to call."

Well, if there's one thing I've learned over the past twenty-five years, it's that there's always an opportunity for new business if you're observant enough to look for it. During a break, I picked up a copy of the *Los Angeles Times* and I went through the paper—the business section, the classified section, the wedding section, the obituary section, every section I could think of—and circled every company that seemed like a possible match for the organization I was training.

As it turned out, I came up with 198 different companies that these sales reps had never contacted before. That's one newspaper, in one day. All of a sudden, there was some new prospecting for these salespeople to work on!

If we're motivated to observe—if we ceaselessly ask ourselves, "What's new about this situation? What can I use to my advantage that I've never seen before?"—then we observe. We find ourselves wondering, "Hey, what do you think I might be able to find in that newspaper this morning?"

In my experience, superior salespeople are superior observers.

Part of observing is being open to new ways of doing things. I've already mentioned the power of reaching out to new prospects by giving speeches and mentioning what you do to your friends, relatives, and acquaintances. Maybe, for you, observing means taking advantage of new opportunities in these areas. (Please note that reaching out via public speaking isn't anywhere near as scary as it sounds, and it can deliver some extraordinary new leads for your sales work. After a recent speech, I walked away with seventy-five new business cards from new acquaintances!)

The point is that you should always be on the lookout for new opportunities for business, whether that means introducing yourself to everyone in sight after a speech or professional function, or mailing a round of letters to customers and prospects, or taking a marker to your Sunday paper to identify new business opportunities. Keep an open eye—even when you're off duty!

Many of my best sales reps carry small pads of paper with them at all times—weekdays, weekends, whenever—exclusively for the purpose of jotting down names of companies they notice. Perhaps they pass a billboard, or see an ad on television, or notice an article in the newspaper. Later, they call their "pad companies" and try to set up appointments. If you make a habit of being observant in this way, then you'll never fall into the trap of believing that there's no one new to call.

Strategy #90

Ask about the Cow

Let's suppose you walk into my office and you notice that I've got a large brown cow in front of my desk.

You don't know why there's a cow in my office, but there is. Not a picture of a cow or a statue of a cow, mind you, but a real, live, big, brown cow. I notice you looking at the cow and I mention that I've had the cow in my office for the past two years. Now, right off the bat, you don't know anything more about why this cow has taken up residence across from my desk for that period of time, but you do know one thing: having this cow on the premises makes sense to me for some reason.

If having a cow in my office didn't make sense to me, what would I have done? Gotten rid of it!

So why would I have a cow in my office? Let's think about some of the reasons. Maybe I like fresh milk; maybe I find the sight of the cow relaxing; maybe I like the "moo" sound it makes from time to time. Whatever reason I've chosen, though, you know that it makes sense to me.

So let's assume that you sell cows for a living. And let's assume that you don't know which of the reasons we looked at is the one that best describes the reason I've got that cow in my office. Before you start talking to me about how great your cows are, what kinds of questions should you be asking me?

The successful salesperson will ask questions like these:

- Why a cow?
- How did you get that cow?
- How did you decide to put a cow in your office?

The mediocre salesperson will ask a question like this:

- What don't you like about that cow?

If I didn't like the cow, I would have gotten rid of it already! Other dumb questions include: "What do you like about that cow?" And some mediocre salespeople won't even bother asking anything at all. They'll just unfold a brochure about the type of cow they sell, smile, and read it, word for word, to the other person while the cow the person selected is sitting there, chewing away at the carpet earnestly.

"Gee, I notice there's a big cow in the middle of your office."

"Yep. I had that cow shipped in here about three months ago."

"Hey, that's great. You know, our cow gives more milk than the cow you've currently got in your office!"

What if I'm lactose intolerant? What if my cow is there to relax me? Or to serve as a conversation piece? Or to impress an important client who visits me regularly and has a mania for taking pictures of cows? All that talk about milk won't make any difference to me!

Unsuccessful salespeople don't ask meaningful questions, or don't ask questions at all. They try to close from the moment they walk in the door, and they respond to virtually everything the prospect says with some variation of, "Hey, we've got just what you need," even though they know virtually nothing about what the prospect does.

As abrasive as it is, and as uncomfortable as it makes the vast majority of prospects who encounter it, this kind of selling will result in sales sometimes. But it won't deliver as many sales as you deserve.

The more efficient selling cycle is driven by your willingness to ask questions—about the past, the present, and the future—and thereby move the sales process forward.

- Gee, what made you decide to put a cow in your office?
- How long have you been using live cows as a stress management tool?
- How did you decide that stress management is important to your organization?
- Have you ever considered using other types of stress management tools?
- Which ones?
- Why did you choose that kind of stress management tool before you put the cow in here?
- What happened when you tried to take that approach?
- What other stress reduction strategies have you been considering for your employees?

Sales reps who don't ask questions but assume from the get-go that they know exactly why the cow is sitting in the office aren't the kinds of salespeople who emerge as superstars. Sales reps who admit that they don't have all the answers ask lots of questions about the past, the present, and the future—in addition to appropriate how and why questions—and they are likely to be highly successful.

Strategy #91

Always Try to Move the Sale to the Next Step

When I give seminars, I always outline the four steps of the sales cycle for the participants—and then I ask them, "What's the objective of the first phase?" And inevitably people say things like:

- "The objective is to get the order."
- "The objective is to meet the person face-to-face."
- "The objective is to understand the customer."
- "The objective is to ask questions."
- "The objective is to close the sale."
- "The objective is to establish rapport."
- "The objective is to plant the seeds for a future relationship."

All of these answers are common. And all of them are wrong.

The objective of each phase in the model sales cycle is always to move ahead to the next phase. When you're opening, the objective is to get the prospect to agree to move forward into a meaningful interview phase. (We call this kind of assent "playing ball.") When prospects are in the interview phase, the objective is to get the

240

prospect to help you track down the information necessary to develop a presentation that fits the prospect like a glove. (That's the longest part of the whole process.) When you're in the presentation phase, the objective is to conduct it so well that the prospect agrees to become a customer when you say, "It makes sense to me—what do you think?" (That question, of course, marks the fourth and final phase.)

Recently, I was running a training program at a major investment house, a company that sells to customers known as very high net worth individuals. I sat down with one salesperson and had an interesting discussion. He was explaining how well he had done in a meeting with one particular individual with a high net worth. I asked, "When are you going back to see the person?" because the strategy is to return to see the person. He said, "Steve, I've got that under control." I said, "That's great! What are you going to do?" He said, "Well, I have to get information from her first, that is I have to get her statements from her other investment house. And as soon as I get that, then I'm going to go back and make my appointment. So I feel pretty secure about that."

I said, "That's fine. By the way, did you give her the special envelope, so she can send back the information, or so you can pick it up when it's ready?" He said, "Well, no, I haven't done that yet. I haven't even thought about that." I said, "Well, let me ask you a question. Did you talk to her assistant? After all, here's a person making, what, $10 million a year? She must rely pretty heavily on her assistant to keep track of everything. Did you mention to the assistant that you'll be back when the statements are in?" "Well, no. I didn't do that either." Then I asked, "When do monthly statements typically come in?" "Usually during the first week of the month." There was a long pause. This conversation was taking place on the twelfth of the month.

I said, "So what are you doing now?" He said, "I'm waiting for this person to call me. You know, it's a little late in the month, but she'll call. I'm sure she will. She told me she would call."

She didn't call. She never called. He never got that sale.

At my company, our definition of a prospect is somebody who's playing ball with you. A prospect is somebody who is going to answer your questions. Ask yourself: Who answers questions about the large brown cow? Who answers questions about coming back? Who answers questions about what they're doing and how they're doing it, when they're doing it? If you can't get a commitment for a specific next step of some kind, either on your part or the other person's, then you're not dealing with a prospect.

So what strategy can you use to advance the sale? The first and most important one is always ask for the next appointment at the conclusion of a face-to-face meeting. No matter who you are, no matter where you are, no matter when you're seeing the person, ask for the next appointment. Now, inevitably people say, "Well, Steve, it's a bad time to ask for an appointment. It's just before the holidays, just after the holidays, just before the summer, just after the summer, just before the winter, or just after the winter." They give a million reasons they can't ask for the next appointment. I can only tell you one reason you should: To find out whether the person is interested in playing ball with you. If you run into someone for whom it's always a bad time, there's a problem somewhere.

Successful salespeople move the sales process forward, and they typically do this by closing each meeting with a request for a specific appointment for the next meeting. Some salespeople say, "Steve, how can I ask for an appointment? I've got no reason to come back yet!" Sure you do! Here's what my own top performing sales reps say at the end of their appointments: "Mr. Prospect, I have an idea. What I'd like to do, instead of ending right now, is think about everything you've told me and look over all the notes I've taken today. And over the next week, I'm going to put together an outline of what we might be able to do for you, and I'd like to come back in a week and show you what our thinking is."

At that point, you are in essence throwing the ball out to the contact. (You'd be doing the same thing if you asked the prospect to meet with one of your technical people the following week to discuss the issues that have come up during your first meeting.) Your contact can either catch the ball, or he can deflect it, ignore it, or let it fall to the ground. In either case, you'll know what's going on.

Don't get too excited about how well your first appointment goes. The most difficult thing is getting in the second time or the third time. It's no sin to get shot down after a first appointment. (After all, as we've seen, it's relatively easy to get!) The real sin lies in not knowing where you stand at the end of that first appointment.

Remember, the objective of the first step is to get to the next step, and that's all you want to do in each and every case. The only thing you should say to yourself when you evaluate your prospect is, "Have I advanced my sale?" If you have not, then you are not playing ball with your prospect, nor is your prospect playing ball with you.

Recently, I had a sales representative tell me a story about a visit he made to someone who occupied a very high position within the target company. This was a woman who's been working side by side with the president of this company for sixteen years. The president trusts her implicitly and works with her day in and day out. But when this sales representative asked, "Can I come back next week to visit the president of the company?" The woman said, without missing a beat, "Well, I'll tell you the truth. He's been visiting our West Coast offices, and I don't know when he's going to be back in the office. Why don't you let me call you about how we want to proceed with this."

They've been sitting across the same desk for sixteen years. Don't you think that she knows when he's coming back from his trip to the West Coast? Of course she does. What she's done is chosen not to play ball. How do you respond to something like that? Well, you can either write a letter and follow up with a phone call asking your contact to review your preliminary outline, or you can have your manager call up a week or so later, so that manager can say, "Gee, did Jim do something wrong? I really think it would benefit everyone if he was able to sit down and talk to the president." Whatever you do, you should try to move the process forward—not leave the appointment in limbo. And if nothing happens after two or three attempts to move to the next phase, you should accept that you're not dealing with an active prospect and move on to some new opportunity.

Successful salespeople know that you have to have the prospect involved in your sale. You simply cannot sell by yourself. The prospect needs to work with you, and you have to take action at appropriate points to help move the sales process forward. What's more, when your prospect bails out, you need to be aware of that!

Strategy #92

Replenish Your
Prospect Base Intelligently

Prospects have a way of evaporating while we're not looking. Let's take a look at exactly how that happens.

Say you have twenty prospects, and your closing ratio is one in five. You make one sale, and actually lose a total of five prospects. One person becomes a customer and the others are no longer valid. You've actually lost five. Yet the typical salesperson will say to himself, "Well, I made one sale. That means I have nineteen prospects to go." No. You only have fifteen!

Then most salespeople go out and take that fifteen, thinking that they are really nineteen, and make another sale. Now they've made two sales and they think that they have eighteen prospects left, but in fact they only have ten, because they've lost—or will soon lose—ten prospects in making those two sales.

To put it bluntly: You can't ease up on prospecting once you've made a sale. After you close a sale, it's more essential than ever that you replenish your supply of prospects. So your daily activity plan has to be driven by prospecting.

Write this down on a card and post it somewhere where you can see it every day: "I need to prospect on a regular basis, and that should be the key to my plan."

Take a look at the number of prospects you have now that you think are almost ready to close. You need to see these people just once or twice more; you're going to have their business, and you know that. In fact, you're willing to bet money on it. My guess is there's not much more to do on those prospects, yet, if you're like most reps, you're spending proportionally more time worrying about these people than you will about developing those who are in the early stages of the game. Plan your day around those prospects with whom you're building new relationships.

Successful salespeople commit to prospecting every day—or something very close to it. That's where they know their time first needs to be spent.

When you plan out your agenda for your day, you should ask yourself: How much time should I allot for prospecting? Not servicing. Not making calls to existing accounts. Not making calls to people who are going to close. Not confirming appointments. All those tasks may be important, but they're not as important as prospecting. That should be first on your list.

I'm talking about making a commitment to develop brand new appointments each and every day you show up for work. I'm talking about prospecting, typically for an hour or so, and typically at the beginning of the day. Even if you say to me, "But my job is to sell to existing accounts," I've got a question for you: When was the last time you sat down and prospected an existing account—tried to find new business within an account that's already buying from you?

Salespeople who plan their day around prospecting are, by and large, successful salespeople. So that has to be your number-one priority.

Strategy #93

Look at the Lights of Two Cars Ahead

The other day I was driving on the Long Island Expressway and something awful almost happened. I was able to avert an accident because I was looking, not at the car in front of me, but at the car two cars in front of me. I saw those brake lights go on first, and I stopped in time to avoid slamming into someone.

That's the kind of thinking that's necessary for long-term success in sales. One of the big differences between successful salespeople and salespeople who don't succeed is that successful salespeople are better able to anticipate what's going to happen in the industries they sell to. They understand what's going on in the worlds that affect the worlds their customers live and work in.

You can anticipate and prepare for the obstacles your prospects and customers face. You can read the journals and industry publications that affect key industries in your prospect and customer base. You can develop networks that keep you fully informed. That means you can anticipate the responses you're likely to get. Successful salespeople learn to anticipate the objections or responses of their prospects, and they learn to prepare themselves and their organizations. They ask themselves, "What can I anticipate? What trends are emerging in industries that affect this industry? What's going to happen two car lengths ahead of me?"

When was the last time you revised your sales materials, based on new information you received from an industry trade magazine, a discussion with a key contact, or an update from the Internet? Sure, your company gives you materials, but there's no law preventing you from setting up revised versions or updating copy. And there's certainly no law preventing you from changing the questions you ask or the order in which you ask them.

The successful salesperson stays informed and constantly updates his or her anticipated sales dialogues and materials as a result of what he's learned. The successful salesperson doesn't wait for change to happen, but rather anticipates change and makes a habit of looking two cars ahead.

Strategy #94

Ask "Does This Make Sense?"

Many sales trainers will tell you never to ask a question to which the prospect could respond negatively or use as a platform to express dissatisfaction with where we're going in the interview. I think that's a load of garbage.

I've already spoken in this book about the importance of being able to ask your customer for help. (In my experience, the number one way successful salespeople do that is by being willing to say, "Hey, I must have done something wrong here. I'm sorry, please let me know where I slipped up.") What I'm asking you to look at now is the superior salesperson's willingness to ask questions that monitor where the sale is going before there are problems like missed appointments, flubbed presentations, and sudden, mysterious consultations with committees you didn't know existed. By asking the right "How am I doing?" questions as the sale progresses, and by physically writing down the answers you receive, you can substantially increase the likelihood that you'll stay on the right track with your prospect.

Let's say you're out driving, and you're not sure how to get to your destination. If you pull in to a gas station, roll down the window of your car, and ask the attendant how to get to West Bumbleton, there's a very good chance you're going to get one of those answers that isn't an answer at all. I don't know what your experience is in that situation, but my experience is that I'm very likely to hear something like this: "West Bumbleton, eh? Well, there are a lot of ways you could do that."

Well, you're in a hurry. You don't want to know a lot of ways. You just want to find out the best, quickest way to get to West Bumbleton. What I've learned to do helps the gas station attendant focus in a little more clearly. I say, "Listen. I've got a wedding to get to. Can you help me out? I want to get to West Bumbleton. Is it this way (pointing to the left) or is it that way (pointing to the right)?" And invariably the attendant says something like, "No, no. It's that way (pointing straight ahead)."

In a similar way, at various points in your discussion with a prospect, you're going to let the prospect correct you by presenting a couple of hypothetical options—assumptions you want to test by letting the prospect be right. (Remember, when the prospect corrects you, everyone wins!)

"So, can I assume your customers use standard-sized widgets to get their job done, or do they prefer the extra-large variety?"

"Actually, most of our customers use very small widgets."

"Oh, okay, small widgets."

And you write "small widgets" down in your notebook. (By the way, I can't overemphasize the importance of taking good notes throughout your meetings with prospects. It gives you the information you need, encourages the prospect to open up, and raises the status of the prospect you're interviewing.)

Prospects and customers love to correct salespeople. So let them—and encourage them to do so throughout the sales process.

Another, perhaps more direct way to put this principle into action is simply to say, "Am I right about so-and-so? Does this make sense?" That kind of question is likely to get you both a reaction and some new information.

"So, Mr. Smith, does what I'm talking about make sense?" Don't save that question for the closing phase! Ask it before you put together your preliminary proposal. If what you're talking about doesn't make sense to your prospect, then you can ask, "Okay, why not? Where did I take a wrong turn?" And, nine times out of ten, your prospect will say, "It's nothing you did, Jack. Here's what the problem is . . . ."

Be ready, willing, and able to ask some variation on "Does this make sense?" throughout the sales cycle. Then carefully record the answers you receive.

Strategy #95

Put the Prospect's Interests First

I honestly enjoy doing what I do. After all these years of selling and speaking—and I've spoken before 9,000 groups now—I still have a blast doing my job. I have a sincere interest in knowing about what people do and why they do it, and I think that comes through to the people I work with and the prospects and customers I interact with every day. I want to find out how I can help people do what they do better.

I don't think it's any accident that salespeople who experience high levels of success in their careers generally don't have to fake it through their discussions with customers and prospects. The stereotype of the salesperson may be the fast-talking used car salesman who manipulates people, but the reality is that people who do well in this profession don't come across as being eager to take advantage of anyone. They simply have a blast doing what they do for a living, and they genuinely enjoy talking about the pluses and the minuses of what they sell. They're sincere. They can be trusted.

The word sincere comes from the Greek derivative of "without wax." Centuries ago, when a clay pot was broken the owner would repair the vessel with wax and keep on using it. The pot was usable, but it wasn't perfect. A really valuable pot was without wax; in other words, it was still perfect. To be a successful salesperson today, I think you must need to make sure your positive values support your actions seamlessly—that there's no wax, no gap, between what you say and what you do.

I've had situations where I had to step back from a situation and tell a prospect or customer, "Wait a minute. What's your objective here? What are you trying to get accomplished in such-and-such an area?" And the answer I received led me to believe that what the organization was after wasn't sales training or motivational training, but advanced management training work that we simply didn't offer at that time. I lost the sale—for a while—because I was honest about what my company could and couldn't do. But I kept an alliance. And I kept my integrity.

I always tell my salespeople that I would rather see them lose a sale because they were sincerely interested in the person's long-term interests than win a sale that subverts those interests. If they come to realize that this was the wrong product or service for them, it's better to be honest and to walk away than to make a sale that really does not help the prospect. That's what top-notch salespeople do, in my experience. They have enough experience, and enough integrity, to say, "You know what? I really don't think this is right for you. I think you're looking for such-and-such, and unfortunately, we don't offer that. But I can point you toward someone who does."

You have to have an underlying belief and sincerity in what you're saying in order to be successful. If you don't believe in what your organization is offering to consumers, then you should go find some-where else to work. If you don't believe in your ability to find the best answers for your prospects and customers, or you can't tell them the truth throughout the process, then you shouldn't be in sales!

Put the prospect's interests first. You'll never regret doing so.

Strategy #96

Prospect Effectively

There are four steps to the appointment making process that takes place during a cold calling (or prospecting) call. The first is the opening, the second is the response the person gives you, the third is the turnaround that you're going to come up with, and the fourth is actually setting the appointment. The problem is that most salespeople spend an inordinate amount of time worrying about what they are going to say in the opening. They think that if they can find a nifty grabber of an opening statement, they can forget about the work in the other three steps. The reality is that sales doesn't work that way.

Of course, you do have to begin with a compelling opening statement that sounds (and is) intelligent. It can't sound phony or unrealistic. Most salespeople start off with a statement that sounds something like this: "Good morning, Mr. Jones. This is Mary Smith. The reason I'm calling you is so I can talk to you about the strategies I have for saving you a million dollars by next Monday morning." In other words, they incorporate claims that are so ludicrously exaggerated that they turn the prospect off almost immediately. (Would you believe someone who said something like that to you before they knew anything about what you do?)

A better statement might be about work that you've done successfully for somebody else. So a typical cold call from one of my top salespeople would open with something like the following: "Good morning, Mr. Jones. This is Mary Smith from D.E.I. Sales Training. The reason I'm calling you today is that a couple of months ago, I finished working with the XYZ company, and I put together a program that increased their sales by 42 percent this quarter over last year. What I'd like to do is stop by next Tuesday at 3:00 and simply tell you about the success I've had for them."

What you do by using that kind of statement is to create a meaningful basis for a conversation based not on what you can do for the prospect (about whom you now know little or nothing), but on what you've done for someone else. That's a realistic foundation for future discussions.

What happens next? Should you expect the prospect to start asking questions about your work with XYZ, or congratulating you on the great results you were able to deliver? Well, that's nice when it happens, but you should probably be ready for some other outcomes, too. The prospect is going to respond to you, and that response shouldn't take you by surprise.

The most successful sales reps know that the responses that arise out of a statement like the one you just read are usually going to have some connection to what the prospect does. Not what you do, but what the prospect does: "We don't do sales training." "We handle all that in house." "We don't use trainers we haven't worked with before." "We just have absolutely no interest." A superior salesperson is going to effectively turn that response around by saying something like this: "You know, Mr. Smith, that's exactly what a lot of my customers said to me before they saw how our programs could complement their existing training programs. What kind of

255

in-house programs are you conducting now?" In other words, you use their response to focus in on one of the questions about what the prospect's company is doing right now.

After you listen carefully and jot down the information you receive, you're going to repeat your request for an appointment: "You know, Mr. Smith, based on what you've told me during this call, I really think we ought to get together to talk about this in person. How's Tuesday at 3:00?" Sometimes, thank goodness, you'll hear the prospect say, "Okay. Tuesday sounds good."

If you conduct your prospecting calls in the way I've laid them out above, and you do it consistently—devoting perhaps an hour every day to the process—then you'll get the appointments you need. No doubt about it.

As I've mentioned, I prospect on a regular basis, and so do my own salespeople. Each and every day that I'm not in front of a group, I will pick up the phone and make fifteen calls. I get through to seven people and set up one new appointment a day. I do this five days a week, so I'm averaging five new appointments a week. My closing ratio is one out of eight; for every eight appointments I make a sale. I bring in fifty new accounts a year. Those are my numbers. What are yours?

Prospecting makes all those ratios happen. It's the activity that gets the whole process started. If you skip it, or wait until your current business dries up, then you're riding for a fall. If you make a commitment to do a little bit of prospecting every day, then the first part of your ratio is in place. Then you can look at every other link in the chain and ask yourself, "What needs improving? What would happen if I scheduled one more appointment per week? How would that affect the whole structure? Or perhaps I could improve my interviewing and develop better presentations. If I worked more closely with prospects, found a way to tailor my presentations more to their situations, could I close one more sale per month as a result?"

Prospect every day—and keep an eye on your numbers. Where appropriate, set new targets for yourself. Develop a set of targets that makes sense for your industry and your income goals and then commit to the front end of your sales cycle by making the calls you need to make, day after day, no matter what.

Strategy #97

Follow the Nine Principles of Cold Calling

Here are the nine proven principles that will support a successful cold calling campaign in virtually any industry. Follow them!

1. Rather than set a daily "number-of-dials" goal, set the goal for the number of first appointments you want to maintain AT ALL TIMES. As you learn more and more about your conversion ratios, make the adjustments that make sense for you to achieve your activity and income goals.

2. Make cold calls daily with the objective of setting at least one new appointment every day. This does not include networking meetings. Block the time out and call for an uninterrupted period. Don't send e-mail or receive incoming calls during that block. Approach this activity with discipline and a sense of urgency.

3. Begin tracking your dials, completed calls and appointments set on a daily basis right now. Compile your results daily. Benchmark your activity to assess your success and help determine your true ratios.

4. Do not stop dialing if you are not meeting with success. Stand up, take a break, practice, reread this article . . . do whatever you have to do, but

don't stop. If you are calling within a particular industry and are finding appointment making tough, diversify your leads.

5. Always be prepared to cold call. Have an identified lead list ready with you always and use it when you have unexpected time available. Don't let organizational issues get in your way. Do not research or prioritize your calls between calls—your calling time is your peak sales time! Do that work "off-peak."

6. Learn the appropriate third party references. Briefly reference your company's past and current success stories, but don't let a lack of complete knowledge keep you from making calls. Don't promise you can do the same thing for this prospect as you did for the ABC Company. Instead, ask for a meeting so you can learn more about the person's unique situation and share what you did with ABC Company.

7. Practice each aspect of the calling process until you are comfortable and confident with your approach. Prepare for the specific objections you will hear and be more ready to turn them around than the other person is to brush you off. Say, "You know, a lot of people told us that before they saw how we could . . .."

8. Ask directly for the appointment. If you haven't asked for one meeting at one specific date and time during the course of the call, you aren't doing it right.

9. Never stop reminding yourself: Sales come from prospects and prospects come from appointments.

Strategy #98

Use Fallbacks

A while back, I found myself in Dallas, Texas, working with a high-tech company. I was looking at notes that detailed people whom the company's sales representatives had called without making a sale. I went through page after page of notes, and I kept noticing that, for the most part, the space labeled "Comments" read simply "Did not buy." So I started to inquire a little bit further. I tracked down some of the salespeople who had filled out the sheets, and I asked, "Mr. Smith here, we've got him marked down as 'Did not buy.' Why didn't he buy?"

For the most part, there was no real reason why any given prospect didn't buy. All I would hear was, "He wasn't interested." Then I'd ask the rep what the company's focus was—what it did during the course of the average day, how it kept its customers happy and its competitors baffled—and reps often had no idea!

These lists of literally thousands of "no interest" companies were in fact particularly promising "fallback" opportunities—rejects from weeks or months past that were definitely worth another call now. I know because I called that list of "no" answers myself, and I closed 10 percent of the people on the list!

Part of the reason the prospects I spoke with were more responsive to me than they had been to the earlier reps was that I did a little bit better job of interviewing than the other people had. (For instance, I asked questions like, "How are you handling such-and-such now?" and "I'm just curious, why didn't you buy from us last time around?") But that wasn't the whole reason I was able to sell to that group. The truth is, rejects don't stay rejects forever. Time passes. People leave jobs or get promoted. Competitive challenges shift.

You and I can increase our sales totals by 5 to 10 percent simply by using the so-called rejects I prefer to call fallbacks. When we hear a "no" from a prospect, it often means only that the prospect has decided not to buy from us right now—not that the prospect has decided not to buy anything, ever, from anyone, at any time. For example, if your prospect's company cannot exist without widgets, they're buying those widgets from some supplier. It may not be you, but they're buying from somebody. If you're a long-distance seller, the prospects you deal with are almost certainly buying long-distance from somebody; it just may not be you. So when you hear "No, we're not interested," what that may really mean is, "We're pretty happy with what we've got right now, and we haven't experienced any catastrophes with it recently, so we don't feel like talking to you right now." Who's to say things won't have changed four or five weeks after your call?

After a sufficient amount of time, let's say, for the sake of argument, three months, call your "old" prospects back and find out whether the same person you spoke with last time is still in charge of buying what your company sells. If you reach the same contact, say something like the following: "Listen, I understand you didn't buy from us six months ago, but I'm just calling today to find out how things are going in your widget acquisition department, and to see if you have any new projects up and running." If the contact has changed, you can start over with the new person.

Now, you're not going make every sale. But by using your fall-backs, you're going to find that you'll increase your revenue totals significantly. As I say, my experience in working with salespeople who use this strategy is that they can expect to do between 5 and 10 percent more business.

You'll recall that earlier in this book, I recommended that you understand when to retreat. Once you've retreated for a few weeks, you should understand when an advance is in order! Don't just let your prospects sit dormant forever! Go back and check on the status of the industry, of the organization, of your contact. A year or so ago I went out on an appointment to meet with a gentleman named Alan who worked at a major oil company in California. I sat down with Alan and had a very good meeting with him, but a few weeks later, I found that, despite several attempts to reconnect on my part, Alan would not return my calls. I retreated from the sale, but a month or so later, as part of my routine of calling fallbacks, I called him up and left a dramatic message: "Alan, would you please call me. I just want to apologize for what I've done." (You'll remember that earlier in the book we examined how effective it can be to take full respon-sibility for the sales process. That's exactly what I did.)

Alan called me back not twenty minutes later and said, "Steve, you don't have to apologize. I've been promoted. I'm no longer in that position and I haven't been checking my voice mail on that extension. Here's the name and the number of the new person you need to talk to. Tell him I said he should get together with you." In other words, because I revisited a dormant account, there was a dif-ferent situation and, eventually, some new business for my company.

Too many salespeople assume that a prospect who says no (or doesn't say anything) has dropped off the radar screen forever. It's not true! Successful salespeople revisit their fallback prospects on a regular basis—a schedule that makes sense based on the industry they work in and the customers they serve. That's not the same thing as calling back every two days and making the receptionists feel queasy when they hear your company's name! Intelligent use of fallbacks means assuming that "no" means "no for now," and scheduling a time for an intelligent status check call at a later point.

You can get creative when it comes to calling fallback opportunities. I've worked with reps who've gotten great results by saying, "You know, Mr. Jones, we were having a sales meeting and your name came up and I was thinking that you and I haven't talked in a while." Or if they have to leave a message, they'll simply give their number and say, "Please tell Mr. Smith I was just thinking about him and wanted to talk to him for a moment."

Try it yourself. You may be surprised at how well fallback prospects react to that simple statement: "I was just thinking about you."

Strategy #99

Know Your Ratios

Is sales a "numbers game?" If sales is any kind of "game," it's a game of ratios. Successful salespeople begin their sales work with a thorough understanding of their own ratios, and they develop a deep understanding of the many ways they can improve on their ratios. Such as:

- How many dials does it take you to generate one discussion with someone who could give you an appointment?
- How many discussions does it take you to generate one first appointment?
- How many of your first appointments are moving forward to second appointments?
- How many in-person visits does it take you to generate one sale?
- What is the average dollar value of each of your sales?

Those are the numbers to watch. Obsessively monitoring and improving on those numbers is how superior salespeople excel.

Successful salespeople know how to find the very best ways to turn strangers into prospects, prospects into appointments, and appointments into customers. They realize that there's more than one phase to the sales cycle, and they keep an eye out for the best ways to maximize their effectiveness during each and every aspect of the unfolding relationship. This book contains some of the best ideas I've encountered over the years for maximizing sales effectiveness throughout the sales process. I think that if you follow its advice, it will help you to improve on your ratios.

I hope you've gathered by now that the selling model I teach focuses on asking people what they do, understanding fully how they do it, when they do it, where they do it, who they do it with, and why they're doing it that way, and then helping them do it better. That's right: Our basic job as salespeople is helping people do whatever they do even better than they were doing it beforehand.

The basic goal is always to help people do what they do better—by understanding fully what it is the consumer is trying to accomplish. To do that, we have to ask a lot of intelligent questions based on what the prospect is doing now, has done in the past, or plans to do in the future. That yields better information than focusing in on what we think the prospect needs.

Strategy #100

Don't Try to Close

The best closing technique is (drum roll) . . . not having one! People talk a lot about "closing" in sales. Our real objective, though, should not be to "close a sale" based on what we imagine the other person needs, but to get people to use our service (forever!) because doing so makes sense to them.

After all, people don't buy because of what we think they "need"—they buy because it makes sense to them to do so, based on what they're trying to accomplish. After all, if they needed our product or service so badly, they would have gone out and gotten it before we bothered to contact them!

So, how do we come up with a plan that makes sense? Many sales reps simply guess. They cover their eyes and hope they will come up with something that matches what the prospect is actually doing. Sometimes what they propose matches. Most of the time it doesn't.

A typical high-pressure "close" tries to manipulate the other person into buying—by, for instance, building up the person's ego, making "concessions" that aren't really concessions at all, or even misrepresenting the facts surrounding the sale, the company, or the product or service. Anyone who's ever seen the movie *Glengarry Glen Ross* will remember the sequence in which Al Pacino tries to retain the money of a customer who wants a refund by pretending to close another sale with a high-powered senior executive who happens to be in the office at the time. (This is supposed to impress the fellow who wants the refund.) Actually, the high-powered senior executive, played by Jack Lemmon, is Pacino's colleague and fellow salesperson; the two are concocting an elaborate charade for the benefit, if that's the word, of their wary customer.

Talk about a "closing trick!" It's a tribute to the realism of the script that this underhanded and manipulative effort to retain a customer with cold feet ultimately fails.

Though outright fraud is (thankfully) somewhat less common in the real world of selling than on the back lots of Hollywood, similarly shady "closing tricks" are still very much in evidence. A number of books outlining such stunts have been extremely successful. Some of the closing lines they feature include:

- "My boss is going to fire me if you don't sign this contract."
- "Here's a pen. Here's a contract. Press hard, you're making three copies."
- "Let's play a game. You write down all the reasons you think you shouldn't buy our widgets, and if I come up with reasons that prove yours don't matter, I win, and you have to buy from us."
- "Did you want the green widgets or the blue widgets?"
- "Let me leave the unit here with you for a week. I'm so sure you'll fall in love with it, I'm willing to bet you'll sign up with us after you see what it can do for your operation."
- "If you buy from me today, I'll win a trip to Hawaii. My family's really counting on that vacation."

The question I'd like to put on the table is, can someone eventually sell something using these manipulative or high-pressure closing techniques?

Sure. In fact, our experience is that you will sell one-third of all the prospects you meet with—no matter what you do—simply because you go out and see enough people. In other words, a good many salespeople sell without gathering a great deal of meaningful information, simply because they show up at the right time. The fancy "closing strategy" they use is more or less meaningless.

By the same token, one-third of the customers who could come your way will decide not to work with you, no matter what you do. You lose these accounts simply because the competition is there ahead of you or because of other problems you can't overcome.

When we step back and look at those two potential segments of our customer base, we realize that one-third is still up for grabs. That's the third we have to concentrate on. That's the third in which our actions can affect the outcome.

There are—and can be—no gimmicks within truly effective selling. There's only good, solid relationship building and a resolute refusal to waste one's time with prospects who aren't likely to buy.

Most sales trainers today still focus on the old objective of "finding the potential customer's need." But I think you can see now why that model doesn't work for me. If you needed a product today, you would go out and buy it, whether it be a copier, a long-distance service, life insurance, or anything else. To sell to someone who's already actively in the market simply isn't a big enough goal for success in today's marketplace. Who wants to count on building a career out of sales that fall into your lap? I certainly don't, and I hope you don't either.

Strategy #101

Start Making Sense

Why do people decide to buy in the first place? Because it makes sense from their point of view. The aim, therefore, is always to develop a plan that will make sense to the other person. We want to win as many of those "top third" sales mentioned in the last chapter as we possibly can, and building a plan that makes sense from the other person's point of view is the best way to do that. But we can't build that plan unless we understand what the other person is trying to do!

To do that, we have to get information about the prospect by asking questions.

Don't imagine you know what the other person "needs." Instead, focus your attention on gathering facts so you can build a plan that makes sense based on what he or she is doing.

The best salespeople have a very simple, very powerful two-phase strategy for initiating new business with their contacts. First, they actively solicit all the objections they possibly can before the close, typically by encouraging prospects to rewrite preliminary versions of their formal presentations. Then, after all the important players in the target organization have signed off on all the key elements of the initial proposal (or "pre-proposal," as we call it in our office), successful salespeople deliver a flawless formal presentation that concludes with the showstopper closing technique to beat all showstopper closing techniques.

They say, "So, Mr. Smith, that's our proposal. I have to tell you, we've spent a lot of time putting this together, and it really makes sense to me. Does it make sense to you?"

That's the closing technique that I've taught top salespeople all over the country to use. I use it myself. I understand fully what the prospect does, and my program honestly makes sense to me after I've worked hard during the interviewing phase to uncover exactly what it is they do and how I can help them do it better.

Now only two things can happen at that point. Mr. Smith is either going to say, "Yes, it makes sense to me, too," in which case I've got a sale, or he's going to say "No, it doesn't make sense to me, Steve." If it doesn't make sense to Mr. Smith, then I don't know as much about the company as I thought I did. (Remember that successful salespeople only close after they've achieved full buy-in on all pertinent aspects of the preliminary plan. If you don't have "go" signals from your decision-makers at the end of your preliminary proposal, you're not ready for a formal proposal yet!)

If Mr. Smith says, "No, this doesn't really make sense," I can pull back and allow myself to be corrected and say, "Well, gee, I must have taken a wrong turn somewhere. I'm sorry. Where did I go wrong in my plan? What doesn't make sense?" Then I take detailed notes on everything that Mr. Smith says (which is something I should have been doing long before I attempted to close the sale).

Closing the sale isn't a matter of spouting a series of magic words that you hope against hope will somehow trick the prospect into buying from you. It's the natural outcome of an extended process during which you listen to what the prospect has to say and propose creative, customized ways he or she can begin to use what you have to offer.

Closing cannot happen if you haven't yet found out what the prospect does! So find out what the prospect does. Take all the time you can to do so. Develop a good plan, one that takes full advantage of the prospect's knowledge and insights. Make sure it's a customized plan, one that is tailored to what your prospect is trying to get done. Then, and only then, you should be ready to say, "It makes sense to me. What do you think?"

Will some people buy from you if you trick them into thinking that your kids will go hungry next week if you don't bring a signed contract back to the office? Will some people buy from you if you manipulate them or play head games? Will some people buy from you simply because you represent a short-term solution to a short-term problem—and they're willing to overlook shameless closing ploys (for now)? Sure. But you won't sell as much as you deserve to, and your customers won't stick with you over time. They certainly won't become partners with you and your organization.

Mediocre salespeople use mediocre techniques, and they achieve consistently mediocre results. Successful salespeople recognize that the foundation for all solid business relationships is trust. They know that they have to earn the trust of their prospects by learning all they possibly can about them, and by only making suggestions that they truly feel are in the prospect's best interest. That doesn't mean they close every sale, but it does mean that every new piece of business they bring in carries the seeds of a mutually beneficial partnership. And when you think about it, that's the very best way to start out new relationships and reinforce existing ones.

May you always be ready to ask the right questions and may the right doors always open for you as you pursue your sales career.

Index

Referrals, 88–91

Rejection, 57–59, 138–42,
219–23

Relationships, 133–34, 224–26

Responsibility, 114–16, 227–29

Retreating, 219–23

Return phone calls, 159–61,
215–16

S

Sales cycle, 46–48, 69–71,
240–44

Sales tools, 2–3, 32–33

Self-analysis, 125–26, 186–87,
208–10

Self-deception, 125–26, 202–4

Self-motivation, 1–4, 101–3

Self-promotion, 95–97

Sharing opportunities, 111–13

Sharing skills, 127–28

"Slapshot" selling, 167–71

Speeches, 108–10

Success stories, 74–75, 122

"Sure things," 54–56, 76–77

T

Top customers, 74–75, 146–47

Tough issues, 156–58

Trust, 14, 16, 66–68, 271

Truth, 98–100

Trying too hard, 39–40

U

Utilization, 2–3. *See also* Sales
tools

W

Worrying, 232–34

Y

"Yes" answers, 194–95

"Yes" follow-ups, 135–37

About the Author

Stephan Schiffman has trained more than 500,000 salespeople at firms such as EMC, Waste Management, ExxonMobil, Motorola, and Nextel. Mr. Schiffman, president of D.E.I. Management Group, is the author of many popular books on sales.

Do you have questions, comments, or suggestions regarding this book? Please share them with me! Write to me at this address:

Stephan Schiffman
c/o Adams Media
57 Littlefield Street
Avon, MA 02322